Your Child
WONDERFULLY
MADE

Discovering God's Unique Plan

Your Child
WONDERFULLY
MADE

Larry BURKETT
Rick OSBORNE

MOODY PRESS
CHICAGO

Moody Press, a ministry of Moody Bible Institute,
is designed for education, evangelization, and edification.
If we may assist you in knowing more about Christ
and the Christian life, please write us without obligation:
Moody Press, c/o MLM, Chicago, Illinois 60610.

The publisher gratefully acknowledges the kind permission granted to reprint the copyrighted material used in this book. If any copyright holder has been inadvertently omitted, that copyright holder should apply to Moody Press, who will be pleased to give credit in any subsequent editions.

All Scripture quotations, unless indicated, are taken from the *Holy Bible: New International Version®*. NIV®. Copyright © 1973, 1978, 1984 by International Bible Society. Used by permission of Zondervan Publishing House. All rights reserved.

The "NIV" and "New International Version" trademarks are registered in the United States Patent and Trademark Office by International Bible Society. Use of either trademark requires permission of International Bible Society.

ISBN: 0-8024-2851-7

1 3 5 7 9 10 8 6 4 2

Printed in the United States of America

Dedicated to

*all the parents who are
struggling to raise their children
in a godly manner.*

CONTENTS

ACKNOWLEDGMENTS

*J*ust as each of us has one body with many members,
and these members do not all have the same function,
so in Christ we who are many form one body, and each member belongs to all
the others" (Romans 12:4–5).

After reading the front cover of this book you might think that only two people were involved in putting together what you now hold in your hands. Leaving you with that impression would be the same as trying to make you believe that it takes the efforts of a senior pastor alone to build and run an effective church. Many wonderfully made and wonderfully gifted people have contributed significantly to the contents of these pages: all of them working in concert, as a body should, with the same ministry motivation.

We would like to take the time here to give honor where honor is due.

Working with Larry Burkett: Thank you, Adeline Griffith, for your work on this book and for your relentless commitment to allow God to use your gifts in support of others. We couldn't do it without you.

At Moody Press: Thank you, Jim Bell. We really appreciate your faith in the project, your input and wisdom, and the summary questions that you wrote for each chapter.

Working with Rick Osborne: Thank you, Christie Bowler, for your many hours working on this manuscript and meticulously and accurately recording our many thoughts, ideas, and stories. Your commitment, your work ethic, and your love for God's work make you a very valuable part of this team (and the reason we made the deadline). Thank you, Ed van der Maas, for your tremendous ability to arrange and order the 50,000 plus words sent your way, for your wit, and for your insightful input. And finally, thank you, Kevin Miller and Ed Strauss, for your aid in research and chasing down the details.

Every book is a team, or body, effort and we are honored to be part of such a talented and committed team.

Larry Burkett and Rick Osborne

INTRODUCTION

Was God intimately involved in the conception and creation of each of our children? Or are they simply wonderful by-products of our marriages?

Does God have a plan for each child's life? Or is it up to our children to choose wisely and make the most of what they have?

How can our children find and follow God's will and plan for their lives?

Can we as parents understand enough about all of this so that we can help our children attain to all that God has for them?

Over a period of years, when I (Larry) was counseling people with their finances, I encountered many who were unhappy in their jobs. They were dissatisfied, unfulfilled, and restless. Later, I started meeting their children, who were struggling to figure out what they should do with their lives and what direction they should take. It was as a result of those experiences that I started Life Pathways, an organization designed to help people find the careers for which they are suited and gifted.

Trying to walk into a career without understanding some basics about yourself and God's plan for you is like walking into a house that has just been framed and trying to figure out where the bedrooms, kitchen, or living room will go. Sometimes it's hard to tell the difference between a walk-in closet and a bathroom. Fortunately the person building the house knows which room is which because there are blueprints.

Anyone involved in the process of building must have blueprints, and the design laid out in the blueprints ties in perfectly with whatever the architect's purpose is for the building. The building is designed to fit a purpose, but simply having access to the blueprints is not enough. Blueprints have to be read and followed, and the building process itself must work. Only then will there be success.

As parents, we often begin to help our children build who they are and who they are going to be without knowing about God's blueprint for their lives, without knowing how to read those blueprints, or without understanding what God's building process is and how it works. As a result, our children, like the majority of us, often end up in positions in life that they're unhappy with and in careers that don't seem to fit who they are.

The purpose of this book is to give parents a glimpse of God's blueprints and how to read and understand them. The goal is that, ultimately, our children will be able to find the wonderful place in life that God has created for them.

In this book we want to help parents understand what the Bible says about God's design and direction for our children. To accomplish this we will focus on three things.

- Explain the blueprint: how God designed us—with personality, character, personality types, uniqueness, talents, and gifting. We present and then set out the differences between these.
- Discuss how to read the blueprint: through understanding God's purpose, calling, guidance, and leading.
- Help parents understand the building process, which involves developing talents and gifting, and finding and following God's direction.

This book starts by laying a foundation for understanding the building process. Then we quickly get into the practical how-tos that will help to guide your children as they develop and grow into all that God has created them to be. To help you in this process we include personality type surveys for you and your children and a unique blueprint-reading system that will help your children map out a career plan that cooperates with God's unique design.

God bless you!

Larry and Rick

Part 1

DESIGN

*"You created my inmost being; you knit
me together in my mother's womb.
I praise you because I am fearfully and
wonderfully made; your works are
wonderful, I know that full well"*
(Psalm 139:13–14).

Chapter 1

WONDERFULLY MADE

Lights blaze. Flashbulbs flash. Photo shoots are organized. Interviews are scheduled. Media representatives jostle for position to ask their questions and get their pictures. Finally, a hush falls as the star walks calmly out onto the stage. Everyone waits for her first word. "Baah!" she says. She sighs and utters a second, drawn-out "Baa-aah."

All the big magazines pick up the story. Our star appears on the March 10, 1997 covers of such prestigious magazines as *Time* and *Newsweek*. Over a period of weeks and months, articles about her appear in a multitude of other magazines, such as *Maclean's, Life,* and *Discover,* as well as a variety of newspapers. She is featured on telecasts and news shows, as debate over her rages. As our star's fame spreads, celebrities maneuver to land photo shoots with her and scientists wangle for interviews and tests.

The celebrity? Dolly C. Sheep. And although she doesn't have much to say for herself, others can talk of little else. What is so great about this unassuming, woolly lady? The middle initial "C" stands for Clone: Dolly is the first mammal to be cloned from an adult cell.

Here's what happened. Each cell in the body has a nucleus that contains a full set of chromosomes for that person—or sheep. A scientist took a fertilized egg cell from a pregnant ewe and removed the nucleus (and thus the chromosomes). Then a new nucleus, from an adult cell taken from another sheep, was put in the egg cell. The cell, which now contained an entirely different set of chromosomes, was implanted in the womb of a surrogate mother sheep. The cell grew like a normal embryo, but the chromosomes in the new nucleus caused the embryo to grow into a duplicate of the sheep from which its nucleus had been taken. Voilà! Our famous Dolly C!

Dolly's laid-back existence caused a media frenzy that overflowed into churches, schools, and homes, as people endlessly discussed the phenomenon. The underlying question that really triggered all this attention: Does the successful cloning of Dolly mean that we could clone humans—that we could "create" 50 Arnold Schwarzeneggers or 100 Princess Dianas or as many clones of a person as anyone might want? If so, where does that leave our understanding of God as the Creator of life? Could we still believe that God is involved in the creation and birth of each human being?

Can human cloning really happen? At least one scientist, Chicago physicist G. Richard Seed, is convinced it can. He sees it as a purely scientific and monetary issue: Either cloning works or it doesn't. If it does, we should clone and use the technology to improve the quality of life. Seed wants to set up a clinic that will clone human babies for infertile couples, thus giving those unable to have babies the joy of having their own (in a very specific sense) children.

When Richard Seed announced his intention, the media once again had a field day. Numbers of articles appeared about the various possibilities this technology raises, from the positive uses for life-extending medical procedures, such as the availability of healthy bone marrow for leukemia patients, to horrible uses, such as cloning headless humans as sources of organs for transplanting.

But the furor wasn't limited to the media. Politicians got involved. President Clinton created a commission that recommended a ban on human cloning for at least five years. He also banned funding for human cloning. To date, nineteen European nations have joined together to sign an anti-cloning treaty.

Richard Seed is not discouraged. He simply plans to move his operations to Mexico or somewhere else. No doubt there are other scientists who feel as he does and who think, "Someone will figure it out and make it work. We might as well be working on it too."

If cloning can produce complete, live humans, are we simply the result of our genetic makeup; or, are we a combination of our genes and our environment? Scientists have studied identical twins to find the answer.

Twin Questions

Identical twins come from the same egg and the same nucleus. They share exactly the same DNA and therefore have exactly the same genetic blueprint. Thus, if humans are simply the result of their genetic makeup, identical twins should be identical in every respect, even if they are separated at birth. For a while, scientists thought they had found proof that this is indeed true.

For example, one of the most renowned cases of identical twins were Jim and Jim, who were separated five weeks after birth and raised approximately eighty miles apart by different families: the Springers and the Lewises. Here are the similarities these twins shared.

Both were dark haired, six feet tall, and weighed 180 pounds.

Both moved similarly, used the same gestures.

Both had owned a dog named Toy when they were children.

Both had married twice: first to women named Linda, then to women named Betty.

Jim Springer had named his firstborn son James Allen.

Jim Lewis had named his firstborn son James Alan.

Both men had had a vasectomy.

Both had worked part time in law enforcement.

Both hated baseball but loved stock car racing.

Both smoked Salem cigarettes, drank Miller Lite, and drove Chevrolets.

Both vacationed on the same half-mile stretch of Florida beach.

Both suffered from migraines and had high blood pressure.

Both habitually bit their nails.

They had nearly identical heart rates, brain waves, and IQs.

Their personality scores on tests were as close as if the same person had written them both.

Stories are told of other identical twins who, though separated at birth (or an early age) and lived a great distance apart, shared not only physical similarities (height, weight, hair color, facial features) but also had the same personal habits, physical infirmities, level of intelligence, and tastes in food. They shared the same favorite color and style of clothing. These things were discovered when they were reunited as adults.

Those are staggering similarities! But what do they really prove? My (Rick's) wife and I both have brothers whose names are Russell. Both of them are firstborn children and both were born in the same month of the same year, within miles of each other. The two of them are similar in many ways. Both of them had wild teenage years, went through a handful of difficult relationships, and, in their thirties, married women who were divorced. They both went to the same high school where they both majored in drafting, and both have mechanical aptitudes. Both also took vocational training.

Both Russells' oldest children are daughters named Ashley. I jokingly told my brother-in-law Russell that if he had another child he would have to have a son and name him Eli, to match my brother Russ. He stopped laughing and told me that just days ago he had told his wife that if he had a son, he wanted to name him Eli. Amazing similarities—but purely coincidental, since the similarities cannot be attributed to a shared genetic blueprint!

Of course, the case of Jim and Jim has turned out to be an exception, albeit a spectacular one.

Studies of identical twins have turned up far fewer similarities. A recent book[1] points out that it is true that identical twins are 90 percent the same in certain physical characteristics: eye and hair color, hairline patterns, blood type, position of teeth, and fingerprint ridge counts.

However, the similarities decrease as we start to consider less physical factors: how they think, feel, and react. Even physical characteristics like height, weight, and complexion aren't as close as we'd expect. When we look at facial expressions and how susceptible twins are to diseases like diabetes, ulcers, breast cancer, and stress, the similarities decrease even more. In short, even in identical twins we see an extensive amount of individuality.

But if these twins are genetically identical, what makes them different? Clearly, genetic makeup doesn't determine everything! The question now becomes, How much of who and what we are is determined by our genetic code—the combination of genes we get from our parents—and how much is shaped by the experiences that have been added to that genetic code by our upbringing? The debate about which of these has more impact on how we turn out is often referred to as the "nature versus nurture" debate: Is our genetic makeup (nature) more important, or is our environment and upbringing (nurture) more important?

There are two extremes to the debate. On the one hand, if I am shaped primarily by my genes (nature), then how I'm raised and the experiences I have are essentially irrelevant to who I am as a person. If, on the other hand, my environment is far more significant than my genetic blueprint, suddenly upbringing (nurture) becomes a very crucial part of how each person turns out. This is because I was a "blank slate" when I was born, waiting for my parents and the experiences of my life to write on the slate and tell me who I am. This would translate to mean that children literally could be molded into anyone their parents (or society) wanted them to be by how they are treated.

The problem is that neither of these theories fits reality. There cannot be an either/or answer to the question of what makes us who we are. The reality seems to be that both nature and nurture are important. But we must take another step. Identical twins raised in the same family, and therefore in the identical environment, *still differ considerably from one another.* Each one of two identical twins is a unique individual, completely separate and distinct from the other. What makes them different? There seems to be a third factor involved in shaping each of us.

God and the Genetic Code

Our secular society has taken its eyes off God, the Creator, and has tried to reduce our existence and who we become to a chemical equation and a predictable process. But it is *God* who originally came up with the idea of a genetic code. He invented DNA and genetics way back when He first made Adam and Eve. In fact, He created the genetic code for the entire human race when He created the first people.

Think about it like this: Your genetic blueprint is a combination of your parents' genetic makeup; your parents' genetic blueprints are combinations of those of their parents', and so on, back through time. Present in the genetic makeup of your grandparents on both sides of your family had to be the genetic combination that would ultimately result in you.

By following this same logic all the way back to the beginning, we can see that when God created Adam and Eve He had already created the genetic code for the entire human race. It was all in Adam's and Eve's genetic makeup. The writer of Hebrews alludes to this: *"One might even say that Levi, who collects the tenth, paid the tenth through Abraham, because when Melchizedek met Abraham, Levi was still in the body of his ancestor"* (Hebrews 7:9–10).

Adam and Eve were, so to speak, the first cell in the body of the human race. In the same way that one cell in our bodies contains the genetic code for every part of our bodies—which is why cloning works—Adam and Eve had within them the genetic possibilities for all the races: the looks, types, colors, shapes, sizes, and the infinite variety of things determined by genes. God created it all within the first cell, the first human genetic code. Everything that a genetic code can dictate was already thought out, organized, and provided for by God.

In actuality then, this means that every single one of us, as far as our genetic code goes, was foreknown and "fore-designed" by God when He made all of humanity in Adam. In Adam lived the genetic code and the possibility for every person who would ever live and for every possible combination of the genetic code that could possibly exist. The sheer number of possible combinations is mind-boggling!

First, there are many possibilities for eggs and sperms in each individual. Each of us has the capacity to generate 10^{3000} (10 to the 3,000 power) eggs or sperm with unique sets of genes. If we consider 10^{3000} possible eggs being generated by an individual woman and the same number of sperm being generated by an individual man, the likelihood of anyone else with your set of genes in the past or in the future becomes infinitesimal.[2]

And, second, each person could marry any of millions of other people with their possible eggs or sperm. Obviously many of the possible combinations have not been and will not be realized. It seems that although the *potential* for our genetic existence was known at the moment of Adam and Eve's creation, God didn't create at that time every person who was going to be created; He only created every genetic *possibility*.

But the design of the genetic code is not the only way in which God is involved. The genetic code is merely the foundation, or the bedrock, of the physical part of a person. To complete that genetic combination and make the person a reality, there's another part that must be added: God's part. The Bible indicates that God takes the physical code and then connects an individual spirit to that foundation when He creates the individual at the moment of conception.

Job said to God, *"Your hands shaped me and made me. . . . Remember that you molded me like clay. . . . Did you not. . .clothe me with skin and flesh and knit me together with bones and sinews?"* (Job 10:8–11).

And Jeremiah affirms that God is involved in forming us in the womb: *"Before I formed you in the womb I knew you, before you were born I set you apart; I appointed you as a prophet to the nations"* (Jeremiah 1:5).

God was involved in creating the genetic code. But He is also involved in creating each human being in each womb individually. God created Adam physically from the dust of the ground. His genetic code was all there. But Adam wasn't alive until God breathed into him (see Genesis 2:7). God was intimately involved in giving Adam life; and, He is still intimately involved in forming each person in his or her mother's womb to give each person life.

*"For you **created my inmost being;** you **knit me together** in my mother's womb. I praise you because I am fearfully and wonderfully made; your works are wonderful, I know that full well. **My frame was not hidden from you** when I was made in the secret place. **When I was woven together** in the depths of the earth, your eyes saw my unformed body"* (Psalm 139:13–16 emphasis added).

David speaks of "my inmost being"—the inner person, thoughts, feelings, moral sensitivity, and so on—in other words, David's spirit. David also speaks of "my frame," meaning his bones or his physical being. What David is saying, then, is that when he was in his mother's womb, God knit together his unique physical being—his genetic code and all the things that code determined he would be—with his spirit, the part that was uniquely him.

God matches the lives of individuals, the spirits of individuals, perfectly to their genetic code and knits the parts of them together in the womb. And He gives them a special place in His heart. No individual is overlooked.

God, the Heavenly Father

When a child is born, most parents are happy—and apprehensive. The joy of parenthood is mixed with a sense of inadequacy, of not being sure that we as parents will be able to do what is best for our children, children that are more important to us than anything. But we can rejoice—and relax. These are not only *our* children being born. These are *God's* children being born, and He is there—present, helping, and creating. He is lovingly involved. Our children are not just a result of us; they are a wonderful combination of a loving union between parents and the love of God, their Heavenly Father.

God pre-designed you and each of your children. He was not surprised by your child's conception. His or her birth did not throw God's plan off track. To the genetic combination created by you and your spouse God added your child's spirit, created by His design. That spirit, designed by God, matched the genetic mix perfectly, so your baby was created to fit perfectly into your family and into the space and time into which he or she was born. With the spirit that God added came all the details of who that person would be and what his or her purpose—God's plan—would be for him or for her. That person was given an identity, a life, natural talents, personality, and everything else that makes a unique individual.

This is the other factor that makes individuals different. Not nature (genetics) alone, not nurture (upbringing) alone, and not some combination of the two can adequately explain all the facts, because we are spiritual beings. It is our God-given spirit, unique to ourselves, perfectly matched to our physical blueprint, that makes us who we are. Science cannot measure nor experiment with the spirit, so scientists try to explain life by using other factors. And they are left with questions.

Deadbeat Dad?

Someone might argue, "That all sounds great." It's wonderful that God knit David together in his mother's womb and designed him.

David is talking about himself. So is Job, and so is Jeremiah. *I'm no David,* you might think; nor are my children. How can we know that these verses apply to every one of us?

Granted, God loves us all. The Bible is clear on that, but many of us don't feel as if God specifically designed us or our children. We might concede that He creates each individual but think that He does it in a less personal, more random, nonspecific way. Okay, He might decide, "Spirit number 4385 gets matched with genetic combination number 4,859,132 this time."

Only periodically does God personally intervene to give us a Moses or a David, a Jeremiah or a John the Baptist. What about us little, ordinary, unremarkable people? Was God really specifically involved in my birth and my life? Is He really involved in the births and lives of my children? Or is God a deadbeat dad who simply can't be bothered to have a deep, personal, Father-child relationship with us?

We can answer in a couple ways. First, it is generally recognized by scholars that it is legitimate for us to take the Psalms as applicable to us. We can see this in how Paul and others applied them to their day and age and to the people they interacted with. Also, God gave us the Bible not simply as history. His Spirit, who inspired it, still breathes life into it as we apply it to our lives. Therefore, Psalm 139 doesn't apply just to David. We may take what David says about God and apply it to our own situations. God inspired David to write what he did, so these verses apply to us, here and now. They are truth for us and our children as much as they were truth to David when he wrote them.

The second answer comes out of our knowledge of the immensity of God's love and ability. His immense vastness, described by the Christian doctrines of His omnipresence, omniscience, and omnipotence, tells us that He is fully capable of intimate involvement in every baby's conception. And in many places throughout the Bible we see God's desire to have a relationship with each person individually. God's love is for each one of us as individuals.

Jesus said, *"Are not two sparrows sold for a penny? Yet not one of them will fall to the ground apart from the will of your Father. And even the very hairs of your head are all numbered. So don't be afraid; you are worth more than many sparrows"* (Matthew 10:29–31).

God's knowledge of us extends even to the unimportant details of how many hairs we have! How much more important is the very creation of who we are as beings and God's involvement in every detail of our lives. He knows everything: past, present, and future. He knows what is going on right here, right now, in every place in the world, both as we write this and as you read it. He knows when you will be reading this. He knows what is going on in the room where you are sitting with this book open before you. He knows what you are thinking and feeling. He knows your questions, doubts, and convictions.

And He has that same intimate knowledge of every other person in existence, all at the same time. He not only has all knowledge, but He also has all power. He could right now speak individually to every one of us. He works in every life, all at the same time. He is at this moment at work in your children's lives.

If He's that vast and that big—which He is—and if His love is more than we can possibly comprehend—which it is—and if His love is His motivation—which it is—and if He created us to have a special relationship with Him, calls us to that relationship, and loves us so much that He sent His Son to die for us—all of which He did—then why would we believe that God somehow is not involved specifically with our creation and cannot or does not have a unique plan and unique design for each one of us and for each of our children? There is nothing to stop Him from doing that.

God is fully capable of designing, down to the smallest details, at conception and in the womb, every baby being conceived right now, around the world, as Psalm 139 says. He is capable. And what we know of His love and character dictates that He is not only capable but also willing.

* * * * *

We started this chapter with Dolly C. Sheep and the frenzy and controversy that surrounded her. The reason why this event is so critical is this: If we can be cloned by science, it would seem that our existence is merely the result of an impersonal genetic combination.

First, let us state unequivocally that we do not condone cloning. In today's world, we seem to think that if something *can* be done it probably *should* be done—and if *we* don't do it somebody else will. But there are limits to what is permissible from God's perspective. Creating a human being is God's prerogative.

Yes, we are involved, but the idea that we can create a human without God's involvement or that we can do it in a way other than the way God created it to work is playing with something that is not a toy. Children are not only ours; they also are God's.

Now that that's clear, let's look at the possible outcomes of a cloning experiment. The first possibility is that God does not get involved and does not give the duplicated DNA a unique spirit—and life is not created.

The second possibility is that God, for the sake of the new life, does get involved and provides a unique spirit for the duplicated genetic code, like He does for identical twins.

A third possibility is an impossibility: that man, apart from God, duplicates not only the genetic code but the spirit of the individual to form an absolute duplicate of an individual. It is impossible, because God is intimately involved in the creation of every one of us, and science cannot duplicate or replace this involvement.

Your children were lovingly and wonderfully made by God Himself. He loves them, they have a special place in His heart, and He has an awesome plan for their lives.

Notes

1. James Hillman, *The Soul's Code: In Search of Character and Calling* (New York: Warner Books, 1997), pp. 130–31.
2. Robert Plomin, J. C. De Fries, and G. E. McClearn, *Behavioral Genetics: A Primer* (New York: W. H. Freeman, 1990).

1. Your child has a genetic blueprint based on a combination of your genes and your spouse's. Which characteristics in your children do you think are most similar to you and which resemble your spouse?

2. How do certain genetically inherited characteristics in your children affect the way you respond to them, either positively or negatively? Do you think you or your spouse may have subconscious responses to these characteristics that bias your view of your children?

3. Most people agree that we should not be judged according to genetic characteristics, such as physical appearance. How then might you judge acceptability, attractiveness, and performance, when these are tied to genetic factors that cannot be changed?

4. Why is it impossible, even with cloning, to duplicate your child? What aspects of your child can never be imitated, recaptured, or duplicated?

5. Reread Psalm 139, a magnificent description of God's creative process and intimate care of us. Pray this psalm back to God, and think of your child's uniqueness as you go through the verses.

6. On an ethical level, genetic characteristics should not affect the way people respond to an individual. But in reality, certain traits or appearances promote acceptance or rejection. Why is this so? How can you work with your children to handle both types of responses to their genetic traits?

7. Name three things about your child that are absolutely unique. How do these characteristics affect the notion that we are all pretty much alike as human beings? Explain to your child that his or her individuality is not a result of random connections; it is a preordained plan on God's part.

Chapter 2

CELEBRATING A CHILD'S UNIQUENESS

One thing that everyone who has two or more children definitely agrees with is that no two children are alike. The dictionary tells us that personality is "the total of the psychological, intellectual, emotional, and physical characteristics that make up an individual, especially as others see him or her." Our children's personalities are who our children are. But it is also their expression of themselves and the perception of that expression by others.

When we look at *similarities* among people, we find that there are some basic personality types—groups of people who share a number of similar personality traits. (We'll talk about this in more detail in the next chapter.) However, when we look beyond the broad similarities, we find that each child, in spite of similarities, is in the final analysis unique—with a one-of-a-kind personality. The mold was "broken" when each of us were made. There is no one like us anywhere in the world now or anywhere in history.

If we think of the people in our families—our children, in-laws, cousins, nephews and nieces, grandparents, aunts and uncles—and all the people we meet at work and church, we would be unable to come up with two identical people. We all react to and approach life differently. We have our own senses of humor, responsibilities, and ways for relaxation. We have unique dreams, expressions, reactions, and ways of speaking.

Take, for example, a child that was playing and accidentally broke a vase. How would that child react? Let's assume we've established in the child's life the understanding of the importance of telling the truth. (We'll discuss this in more detail in Chapter 4, Character.) The child has the confidence that he or she is an honest person and knows what has to be done, so the child will tell the parents what happened. However, the way that child confesses will be completely unique and an expression of his or her personality.

Some children will hang their heads and have trouble making eye contact with their parents, scuffing toes across the rug as they talk in inaudible tones. Others will lift their heads and look their parents straight in the eyes. Still others will start bawling so that it takes fifteen minutes to figure out what they are trying to say as they stutter confessions through their tears. Their eyes, their faces, what they do with their hands and feet, all shout out your children's uniqueness.

One child might make Mom or Dad a nice cup of coffee first. Another might be very matter of fact and say, "Mom, I wasn't supposed to play with your vase. I did. I'm sorry. I've learned my lesson. I want you to forgive me. I know you will, so that's okay. Bye." That child just states the facts, covers the bases, and is off. Another will be deeply remorseful, sharing the sadness at the broken vase. Every single child will do it differently.

All of what God made our kids to be is wrapped up in a single, unique package. The way they each express their uniqueness is part of their personalities. They are different from everybody else in the nuances of how they talk (using only their voices or their eyebrows or their whole faces), the emphasis they put on things, the way they move and think of things, their pet peeves, preferences, likes, and dislikes.

Children differ in what makes them laugh, the things that appeal to them, the things they enjoy thinking about or avoid thinking about, what they know, what moves them, their body language and hand movements—everything about them is part of their personalities. It all shouts out (or for some kids, whispers) to the world, "This is who I am." Their personalities encompass every part of them, idiosyncrasies and foibles included. It's the way they interact with the world around them and how that world sees them.

Your children's personalities are unique but not static. Personalities grow and are shaped throughout their lives as they get older, live, learn, and experience things. And as they face different things, take advantage of opportunities, face closed doors, react to the world and people around them, and choose different ways of approaching life, they continue growing. As they grow, they do it in their own particular ways. They choose to express themselves in new ways. They learn better, more gracious or effective ways to interact with others. All of these things contribute to and at the same time are expressions of their unique personalities.

If God can make every snowflake different and give us all unique fingerprints, He obviously has no trouble making every person different who has ever lived or will ever live. *God rejoices in our uniqueness and in our children's.* He did it on purpose.

As parents we can equally rejoice in our children's individuality. Even in difficult situations we can watch our children and notice how absolutely one-of-a-kind they are. And those unique personalities are wonderful, unexpected, surprising, beautiful things.

Enjoying Our Kids

As parents, we always need to enjoy and rejoice in our children's individuality. This is easy when they're cute and say something in a way that we haven't heard or thought of before, when they come up with something intelligent, or when they're performing "up to par."

But sometimes it's harder. We can easily get impatient with a child who is boisterous, talkative, and always jabbering away about something or other. It's tempting at those moments to say, "Why can't you be more like your sister? She's sitting so quietly reading her book." Or we might be frustrated with our more withdrawn, quiet child, and say, "Why can't you be more outgoing like your brother? He's always outside playing with the neighbor kids." But they *aren't* like their brothers or sisters. They are *themselves*. We need to remember that and enjoy their differences.

This is easier for some parents than for others. All parents have unique personalities of their own as well! Some have the kind of personalities that like to be in control, that plan and want to make sure that everything goes as planned. These parents may have great difficulty rejoicing in a child whose uniqueness expresses itself in unstructured, spontaneous, and often unpredictable ways. Or, parents who enjoy doing things on the spur of the moment may have difficulty understanding their children's difficulty in dealing with uncertainty and need to know ahead of time what's going to happen. God has a gentle sense of humor that seems to express itself in His matching of parents with children! Parents must help their children grow, but God wants parents to grow as well.

As parents we need to be careful not to try to conform our children's personalities to the images we have of "ideal" children. We must not give them the impression that *this* is a proper, acceptable personality while *that* is not. My (Larry's) son Todd is the classic example of this. From birth, he was different. He embarrassed us. I could go through a whole string of stories about Todd that are hilarious.

We struggled for years and years, trying to change him, trying to teach him how we thought a Christian son ought to behave and be—polite, disciplined, well-groomed. But the way we thought "polite, disciplined, and well-groomed" should look or be defined just wasn't Todd. It's not that Todd wasn't any of those things, but he had a totally different way of defining and expressing them. He was wild in church, wore a ponytail, and so on. Our other children conformed much more to what we were comfortable with. We eventually learned to accept and enjoy Todd for who he was. As parents we can do irreparable damage if we try to pressure our children to conform to our own personalities.

It's also important for us to help our children recognize the differences in their siblings and friends. We can help them learn to value these differences and the things that make each person who he or she is. They do things in their own way, and they're naturally good at different things, which doesn't make them better or worse than other people. As we help our children understand this, they learn to value how God made each one. What a unique and wonderful gift each person is!

Training Personality

Personality is wonderful. And although we mustn't squelch our children's personalities or attempt to force them into some other mold, we still need to train them in how they express themselves.

Personality should never be used as an excuse for bad character. A child who misbehaves is showing bad character rather than expressing unique personality. A child who has a strong personality, for example, does not have an excuse to be disobedient. We should never say, "Yes, my son doesn't listen, but that's because he has a strong leader's personality. One day he'll be a leader and God will really use him." Or, "My daughter has an amazing imagination so, naturally, she stretches the truth sometimes." Or, "My twins have great artistic talent; that's why I can't stop them from writing all over the walls, even though I've told them a million times not to." Bad character is simply that: bad character.

We need to be clear with our children that character (as we will see in Chapter 4) is God-likeness. It doesn't change, no matter what our personalities are. Our personalities, however, will express this God-likeness in our own unique ways; but personalities are never an excuse for sin.

We need to train our children in the correct expression of who they are. If our children are leaders, we may have to spend some extra time teaching them what good leadership is. We'll need to show them how obedience and cooperation are important for leaders to learn. We'll need to teach them that having servants' hearts and consideration of others and their ideas result in others being willing to follow them and their leadership.

Personality is not an excuse for bad behavior. For example, we can't say, "That's just who I am. I get impatient and I shout at people." The fruit of the Spirit is the foundation for the positive expression of personality. *"But the fruit of the Spirit is love, joy, peace, patience, kindness, goodness, faithfulness, gentleness and self-control"* (Galatians 5:22–23). Regardless of our personalities, the fruit of the Spirit must be evident in our lives.

Children must be trained in the fruit of the Spirit, with God's help. Along with that goes training in manners and common courtesy (which is becoming more and more uncommon).

If your daughter is very talkative and tends to talk right over other people, you can't just say, "She is such a people person!" You need to teach her to be considerate and listen to others. You need to train your children to be courteous, kind, loving, considerate, gentle, mannerly, and so on.

Personal space is another teaching point. Different personality types have different comfort levels when it comes to personal space. Some people, when they talk, get very close and want to talk just inches away from another person's face. Others prefer a couple of feet between them and the other person. Some people tend to touch an arm or hand when they talk, which may make others uncomfortable. *Our children need to learn to respect other people's boundaries.*

Along this same line is the need to teach our children about *ownership and respect of other people's property.* Some people enter a house and walk around touching the various possessions, or they think nothing of reading over someone's shoulder when that person is typing at the computer or writing. This is an invasion of privacy and can make someone feel uncomfortable.

I can't express my personality all over you, shout in your ears, jump up and down, get all excited, and invade your personal space to the point that you're bothered and then say, "Oh, this is just the way I am. I'm a very friendly person. You shouldn't be bothered by that."

No. We need to train our personalities and tone ourselves down if other people don't like what we're doing. We're all responsible for serving and loving others. So if someone finds our behavior objectionable, we can't say, "You just have to accept me the way I am." If each of us did this, demanding that everyone accept us just as we are, without considering who they are, we would end up with quite a mess!

We all need to learn to be flexible and considerate of whom we're with and think about how we're coming across. There are things about our personalities, the way we behave, that turn other people off, shut them down, and make them not want to be around us. Those are things in our personalities that need to be developed. We need to remember that our personalities aren't just who we are but also how people perceive us.

It's our job as parents to train our children's personalities and how they express their uniqueness. Simple good manners and courtesy go a long way in this. We need to help them learn to express their wonderful individuality in ways that go along with having good character, respecting others, and moving their relationships forward.

Uniquely Related

Not only are our personalities unique, but *all our relationships are special* too. There is a dynamic between two people that is peculiar to that relationship. You and your spouse are each one of a kind. So are your children. But you are different with your spouse than you are with your children. And your relationship with each child is different from your relationship with the other children. Each relationship is good. Each is loving. But somehow each is also completely unique.

Your relationships with colleagues are different from the relationships those colleagues have with each other. People draw different things out of us because of who they are. Every relationship between two people is a unique relationship between two absolutely unique people. It can never be duplicated.

The same is true of God and our children. When God created us and our children as individuals, He knew He would relate to each of us individually and uniquely, even as we love our children individually and in slightly different ways. So, at the same time God created us and our kids, He also created a special place in His heart for us—a place that only we can fill.

Look at the various biblical characters and see their different relationships with God—the prophets, for example. They obeyed their prophetic calls in very different ways. Elijah was one of a kind with his earthy, straightforward ministry, his confrontations with leaders on God's behalf, the frequency with which God enabled him to perform miracles, and his occasional fits of righteous anger.

Then look at Ezekiel. His relationship with God was more visionary, much less down-to-earth (except when he lay on his side for more than a year), and was filled with wild and bizarre visions. Then there was Jeremiah, "the weeping prophet," and Isaiah, who gave us the magnificent messages of Immanuel, of Jesus the Messiah and Suffering Servant of God.

God related to each of these in very different ways, in accordance with their personalities. Their walk with God and their personalities were perfectly suited to God's plan for their lives and the tasks He gave them. We also could compare how God related to Abraham, Jacob, Joseph, and David, Deborah and Samuel, Ruth and Esther—or to the apostle John and the apostle Paul, who were clearly very different, as we can see from their writings.

What this means is of critical importance: *Our children's relationships with God will be different from our relationships with God.* Their relationships with their Heavenly Father will perfectly suit who they are, God's plan for their lives, and what He has for them to do. Those relationships will also grow differently. They may pray in different ways—one may want to talk God's ear off while another has a straight prayer list—memorize the Bible in different ways, and fit in with God's people in different ways.

We need to train our children in the various aspects of developing their relationships with God: prayer, Bible reading, study and memorization, church attendance and participation. But we need to do it in a way that values their individuality and therefore fits with the uniquely designed place God has for them in His heart.

The best place to start this training is at home, with brothers and sisters. Help your children understand that they have unique and special personalities—but so do their brothers and sisters! They should learn to accept that they are all different. They should treat each other with good manners and with respect. They should be polite to each other and respect each other's property and personal space.

Brothers and sisters who learn how to get along with each other and live together not only will have lifelong friends in their siblings but they will be able to make all the other relationships in their lives work. But it goes beyond human relationships. The Bible says that *"Anyone who does not love his brother, whom he has seen, cannot love God, whom he has not seen"* (1 John 4:20). Siblings are the training ground for relationships with people—and with God!

1. In terms of personality, how are your children similar and how are they different? If you have only one child, how is he or she similar to you or your spouse? How is he or she different?

2. Review the story in this chapter of the child who accidentally broke the vase. Which child in the story resembles your child, or children, and why? What does this story tell you about how we need to respond differently to our individual children?

3. What features of your child's personality are most obvious? How have you seen these features grow and change over the years, and how might they be channeled most effectively?

4. What aspects of your child's personality cause impatience in you? What other negative ways do you respond to these aspects, rather than to behavior that is clearly disobedient?

5. As parents, we sometimes make excuses for bad behavior or let our children cross boundaries, because we are not sure how to handle them or don't feel capable. If these situations exist, what can we do to be more effective in disciplining our children?

6. You respond differently to each of your children, whether you realize it or not. Ready for an honesty test? Ask your children as well as your spouse whether or not your responses to your children suit who they are and their particular needs. Discuss their answers, and see how you can change your responses to better suit their personalities.

7. Do a study of Scripture to understand different personality types among biblical characters. What does this teach you about the types of people God uses to complete His varied tasks?

Chapter 3

PERSONALITY TYPES

One of the more memorable moments in *Star Wars* is the cantina scene, in which Luke Skywalker and Han Solo walk into a café that's crowded with alien life-forms, sitting and talking together in rather uneasy harmony to the music of a band made up of aliens. There are aliens with two heads; aliens with elephant-like noses; aliens with huge eyes, several eyes, or no eyes; aliens with various numbers of limbs; and aliens with a variety of protuberances on their heads. Each alien life-form speaks its own language, has its own social customs and priorities, and has its own perspective on life—and on other aliens.

On Earth we have only one fully sentient (aware) species, *Homo sapiens*—us—although at times it seems that men and women are so different that they could almost be alien species. But imagine what would happen if each person were even more different from the next than men are from women! What would happen if we were each as individual and different as the aliens in the *Star Wars* cantina? What if we were all so unique that we could never meet on a footing of understanding with another human? Chaos. And although in this book we have gone to great lengths to show that God made each of our children unique, we also must talk about similarities. God made us the same in many ways so that we can live together in community.

Jesus said the two greatest commandments are *"Love the Lord your God with all your heart and with all your soul and with all your mind. . . . and. . . love your neighbor as yourself"* (Matthew 22:37–39). God is love and, therefore, is totally unselfish. So we know that whatever He asks of us or tells us to do is for our good. That also means that the two greatest commandments carry the two greatest blessings.

The first commandment, to love God, comes with the greatest blessing—relationship with God and having Him as our Father, to love us, guide us, teach us, help us, protect us, and provide for us. The second greatest commandment is that we are to love our neighbors as ourselves. It comes with the second greatest blessing—relationships with others.

Scripture tells us that we are made for relationship. *"The Lord God said, 'It is not good for the man to be alone. I will make a helper suitable for him'"* (Genesis 2:18). God wasn't just talking about Eve, although she was, of course, the start of it. He was talking about the fact that He did not make human beings to be alone. He made us to live in community, starting with our families and moving out from there to communities of all sorts.

"God sets the lonely in families" (Psalm 68:6). This is God's blessing for us. Paul told Timothy, *"I long to see you, so that I may be filled with joy"* (2 Timothy 1:4). He knew the benefit of the support and companionship of good friends. The Bible is full of verses about how we should encourage one another, meet together, and build one another up.

God has placed us with others. He has given us the blessing of being with others, having the chance to get to know all these other individuals He has created, and developing growing, loving relationships with them. God made us individuals, but He also made sure we are enough alike to enjoy one another. We all kind of look alike: we are bipedal (we walk upright on two legs), we have heads at the top and feet at the bottom, and so on. We can all communicate with one another—with varying degrees of success. We all share similar emotions and feelings: joy, hope, love, sadness, peace, and more. God gave us these similarities on purpose.

Personality Types

When we look at the people around us, it doesn't take long before we begin to see that in spite of the uniqueness of individuals there are also patterns of similarities. One of those patterns is personality types. Throughout history, as people have tried to understand each other, theorists have grouped personalities into various categories.

In ancient Greece, more than 400 years before Christ, the brilliant physician Hippocrates first put forth the theory of four types of personalities. He called them *Choleric, Sanguine, Phlegmatic,* and *Melancholic,* after what he believed to be the four main body liquids that were responsible for our temperaments or personality types.

Since then many others have studied people extensively and come up with other categories of personalities. Most systems of personality types still use four basic categories, although the labels differ, and the four basic types are often further divided into eight or sixteen types, since no one fits one type completely but everyone is some kind of mixture of the four basic types.

Life Pathways, an organization that is part of Christian Financial Concepts, Inc. (Larry's organization), has extensively studied personality types and other factors that influence how people fit into career and work situations. After in-depth research and preliminary tests, Life Pathways has developed a survey that is amazingly accurate at describing people's personality types. Many people who have taken their surveys have been shocked to discover how closely the results describe them.

During my (Larry's) twenty-plus years of counseling families, I noticed that people didn't enjoy what they did for a living, weren't really good at it, but were afraid to leave their jobs. I used a DISC test with the couples. It was clear that their personality profiles didn't fit the jobs they were in. For example, a salesperson who is an introvert isn't going to do very well.

If there was a test like this, to determine people's personality profiles, I wondered why there wasn't one to determine people's vocational aptitude, interests, skills, and values that could help steer them in the right career path. I began to see my clients' children making the same mistakes. They had studied the wrong thing in college, gone into the wrong career, and now were trapped in careers they hated.

I discovered that there were several vocational tests. But they were very complicated, had to be administered by professional psychologists, and were very expensive. Then in 1987 I met Lee Ellis at one of our training sessions. He was an ex–Air Force POW fighter pilot, who was getting his master's in counseling. I asked him to come on staff at Christian Financial Concepts to help us develop a test that would be accessible for people and help point them toward suitable careers.

Lee started developing the *Career Direct* test. It took seven years before the test was ready, but we've tested over 50,000 people. I believe we have the largest vocational testing organization in America; we do about 3,000 a month. It is the most accurate, simplest, vocational test ever created. We can't show you what you should do, but we can show you what you shouldn't be doing.

The labels Life Pathways uses for the four basic personality types are *Dominant, Influencing, Steady,* and *Conscientious,* or DISC. These four types reflect four major behavioral tendencies. Most people who take the surveys will score high on two of these and low on the other two, although some people are high in three and others in only one. (By the way, Larry's profile is high D/high I; Rick's is high I/high D.)

Here are brief descriptions of each of the four personality types.

Dominant. People with a high level of dominance (high D personalities) are naturally motivated to control their environment. They are usually assertive, direct, strong-willed, typically bold, and not afraid to take strong action to get the desired results. They function best in a challenging environment.

Influencing. People who are highly influencing (high I personalities) are driven naturally to relate to others. Usually they are verbal, friendly, outgoing, and optimistic. They are typically enthusiastic motivators and will seek out others to help them accomplish results. They function best in a friendly environment.

Steady. People who have a high level of steadiness (high S personalities) are naturally motivated to cooperate with and support others. They are usually patient, consistent, and very dependable. Being pleasant and easygoing makes them excellent team players. They function best in a supportive, harmonious environment.

Conscientious. People who have a high level of conscientiousness (high C personalities, also called cautious) are focused on doing things right. Usually they are detail-oriented and find it easy to follow pre-scribed guidelines. Typically they strive for accuracy and quality and therefore set high standards for themselves and for others. They func-tion best in a structured environment.

How the Personality Types Function in Community

Is it important to know what type or combination of types we are, or is it just an interesting exercise? It is very important indeed. Our per-sonality types show us what we are designed by God to bring to com-munity; God gave us these types so we could work in conjunction with each other. So when we come together as a group, which we often do in order to accomplish some task—whether it is building something, structuring a program, running our community, making a business work, or just having a party—it seems that each person brings with himself or herself a different part of the task. To be effective we need different people who are interested in different parts of the task and who, therefore, will accomplish different jobs. Working together, the task will go smoothly and be a success.

In 1 Corinthians 12 and Romans 12 we see people with different tasks. But we also see people with different motivations. For example, the encourager's motivation is obviously toward the person. The leader's motivation is toward the goal. It's the same with these personality types. Each type has something to bring to the community that is needed in or-der for that community to function well. Each type comes with a *"why"* and a *"way"* (the reason why they function a particular way).

The Dominant Type. The *why* that he or she brings to the group is the passion for the goal, to go ahead, to take the group and go forward to new things. Dominant personalities make sure they have a goal and that they achieve it. They ask, "Are we going forward? Where are we heading?" The *way* the Dominant person does this is by coming up with a goal, leading people toward it, and stirring people to move for-ward. They take charge and help the group move forward.

The Influencing Type. Their *why* is to ensure that everyone gets involved and enjoys themselves along the way. They bring fun into any task. They believe, *if we're going we might as well enjoy ourselves.* They plan the party. They ask, "Are we having fun yet?" The Influencing person's *way* to accomplish this is by being talkative, joking around, clowning, and being the life of the party and a motivator.

The Steady Type. Their *why* is to make sure that every individual is taken care of. They make sure no one is left out or forgotten. They include everyone and see that those who need help are helped. They want to make sure everyone is comfortable with where they're going. They ask, "Is everyone here? Has everyone had a chance to give their input? Does everyone have what they need?" The *way* this is done is through making everyone feel important, welcome, and included. They bring a calm, comforting atmosphere of care and cooperation.

The Conscientious Type. Their *why* is to make sure that we stick to the rules, the tried and tested way. Let's do it right. They ask, "Is it biblical? Are we organized? Are the details taken care of? Is the plan right before we take off? And do we have all the equipment? Have we done it this way before so we know it works?" The *way* they do this is by being organized and studious. They make sure the minutes are taken and the paperwork is done. They take care of the details.

When we put all these together, we can be sure that all aspects of the task are taken care of and that everyone is happy about where we're going and how we're getting there. Without each of these four types of people contributing their part we could easily get lost, stagnate, go for the wrong goal, or end up with people who are unhappy and frustrated. Each of us has a role to play in community, and each of us is needed.

Handle with Care!

Most of us are fascinated with personality types and discovering what personality type we are or where we fit into these categories. And we enjoy trying to categorize the people we know. We take the generalizations of the personality types and start pigeonholing everyone. We can find ourselves saying, "You always do this." or "You're just not good at that."

It is vital that we use personality types with caution. *They are not intended to define us.* They are not for the purpose of saying, "This is who I am." or "This is who you are." They are something God has given to help us understand each other and to function in community. There are as many different personalities as there are people. We are all individuals, and we all fit the personality types in different ways.

We should not use personality types to limit our children. We must not use this to say, "This is your strength and this is your weakness." The child will associate himself or herself with these statements and begin to feel locked in. This could lead the child to a kind of complacency, saying, "Yeah. This is what I do well. But I don't do that well. Too bad."

There are three things we need to teach our children about personality types: (1) what personality type they are and what their strengths are; (2) how they bring those strengths to a group and how they can operate most effectively in a group; and (3) how to recognize, work with, and value other people's types and contributions.

1. What Type?

It's important to help our children understand their strengths and what they have to offer. To do this, we've included in the back of the book (Appendix A) a simple personality survey you can use with your younger children, although you may already recognize them in the descriptions we've given. This survey is from John and Cindy Trent and Gary and Norma Smalley's work. They've done an excellent job explaining personality types for children, using the same general categories as Life Pathways but giving them animal names that are easier for children to relate to and remember. They call the four types *Lion, Otter, Golden Retriever,* and *Beaver* instead of Dominant, Influencing, Steady, and Conscientious.

We also have included a survey suitable for use with older children and teens (Appendix B) and one for adults (Appendix C). Do the adult survey for yourself first and then go through the child's survey with your children. Briefly explain the different types to them (a very brief description is included in the test), and help them understand the strengths of the various types. If you can think of someone your child knows who seems to demonstrate a particular type, you may want to use that person to help explain the type (but resist the temptation to pigeonhole him or her).

Remember, however, to explain to your children that *their types are not a complete definition of who they are*. It simply helps them understand how they most naturally fit into groups and the strengths they have to offer group activities. It is God's design for them to have something valuable to contribute; personality types help us understand what that is. You probably will notice that your child is not completely one type or another. Each child will have some elements of all four of the types but will have a preference, or a more natural leaning, toward one or two of the types.

2. Functioning Best in a Group?

We need to explain to our children how their personality types allow them to function in groups. This includes understanding what their natural strengths are in group settings. Our children need to know that they have something significant to offer and that without their contribution the group will be less effective.

Let's look at the example of planning a summer party and what each personality type would bring to the planning meetings.

The **Lions** would take charge. They would have a good idea of what kind of party they could have. They might suggest a summer fair at which everyone could have a booth with a game or two. They would charge a minimal fee and have food, games, and competitions. The Lions would get people enthused about the fair and start figuring out who could do what. They would lead the meetings to make sure they kept moving toward the goal and would make sure each meeting accomplished something. They would want to make sure, when the time came, that everyone did their part, and they might volunteer to open and introduce the event.

The **Otters** would crack jokes every time they got together. They would make sure the planning meetings were fun and would be the life of the party. They would make all kinds of suggestions for making the fair as much fun as possible and would want as many people as possible there. They might suggest clowns, "funniest pet" competitions, a "dunk the parent" booth, and water balloons. They would volunteer to tell everyone about the fair, do the advertising, and help round up the various acts. The Otters would want to perform and perhaps would plan a parade to let everyone know about the fair. They like to be up front and on stage.

The **Golden Retrievers** would want to open their meetings with a time to catch up on how everyone was doing. They would check to be sure that everyone was there and want to wait if someone was missing. They would want to find ways to involve everyone, including the new kid on the block, and they'd want to be sure that everyone who came to the fair had something to enjoy. They would volunteer to call individuals who might get left out and specifically include them. They'd want to be sure that everyone involved was made to feel that their parts were important. Golden Retrievers would allow everyone a chance to give input and get questions answered, and they probably would smooth over any disagreements.

The **Beavers** would take the notes from the meetings and make sure all the decisions that had to be made were made. They would make sure they all got their minutes and knew their responsibilities. They probably would want to make sure all the equipment was ready for the big day, that everyone knew where their booths would go, and that each booth had enough space. Beavers would ask all the questions: how much would have to be charged, what would be given for prizes, how soon and where the advertising had to be done, who will make sure to get permission to use the arena for the fair, how many booths will there be, how much food will have to be ready, and who will clean up. The Beavers always take care of all the details.

Ask your children if they see themselves in one of these descriptions, and point out to them that each personality type has something important to offer the group. Show them how, if all the personality types do their parts, all aspects of an event or a plan are naturally taken care of. They need to realize each part is crucial to the whole.

"Now the body is not made up of one part but of many. If the foot should say, 'Because I am not a hand, I do not belong to the body,' it would not for that reason cease to be part of the body. And if the ear should say, 'Because I am not an eye, I do not belong to the body,' it would not for that reason cease to be part of the body. If the whole body were an eye, where would the sense of hearing be? If the whole body were an ear, where would the sense of smell be? But in fact God has arranged the parts in the body, every one of them, just as

he wanted them to be. If they were all one part, where would the body be? As it is, there are many parts, but one body" (1 Corinthians 12:14–20).

Children need to be trained how to most effectively use their strengths in a group. There are, for example, several ways to lead. One is to come to the meeting with everything planned, lay down the law— "this is how it is going to be"—without listening to anyone, and then push and shove everyone into "doing it my way."

It's important to have leadership strengths that lead from in front, rather than push from behind, cracking a whip as they go. More effective leaders listen to everyone's input, find out the questions people have, work through the solutions, and bring people to a consensus. Good leaders learn to use the strengths of each of his or her team members. In the same way, children who are very social and outgoing will need to be trained in how to be considerate of others in the middle of their desire to have fun—how to learn to tone it down so that the details can be taken care of, and so on.

Yes, our children have these natural, God-given strengths. But that doesn't mean they automatically have the wisdom for how to use them in the most loving and effective way. It's our job as parents to help them temper their strengths with love and consideration, lining them up with the solid unchanging character they are developing.[1]

3. Recognizing, Working with, and Valuing Other People's Types

It's one thing to recognize how important our parts are to groups, but it's another to understand how important other people's parts are, especially those really different from us. Paul warns us about this.

"The eye cannot say to the hand, 'I don't need you!' And the head cannot say to the feet, 'I don't need you!' On the contrary, those parts of the body that seem to be weaker are indispensable, and the parts that we think are less honorable we treat with special honor. . . . But God has combined the members of the body and has given greater honor to the parts that lacked it, so that there should be no division in the body, but that its parts should have equal concern for each other" (1 Corinthians 12:21–25).

We need to point out to our children that they need to understand other people's functions—the parts they play. The parts that are the most foreign to us may seem less important, but they are equally as important as our parts. We must learn to appreciate and value every person's ability to contribute.

With your children, try to make a game of figuring out what each person contributes to an event, whether it's a birthday party, a Saturday afternoon hike, a shopping trip, or whatever. And then ask them, if this or that part were absent, what would be missing from this event? Be clear with them that no one is only one type, so one person can contribute more than one part. Also, several people can work together to contribute the Beaver's role, for example. Each person has a piece, or part of a piece, or parts of several pieces to contribute.

What would our mythical fair be like without the *Lion's* piece of the pie? Well, there might not be a fair at all. Perhaps, somewhere along the line, the goal would be lost and the planning would go off track. Or no one would know what he or she was supposed to do. The planning might bog down in the need to have fun, in making sure every single person had something important to do, or in getting so caught up in planning the details that no decisions ever get made. The Lion's part is needed to ensure that things keep moving forward and stay on track.

Without the *Otter's* piece, they might end up with a fair, but it would probably be full of boring booths. No one would really look forward to working on the project because it would just be work with no fun. And when the day came, there might not be very many people there because there was no one filling the role of the Otter, spreading the word around and getting everyone excited about how much fun it would be. Without the Otter's part, the planning meetings would be dry and just plain hard work.

If there were no one who could contribute the *Golden Retriever's* part, by the time the fair came around there probably would be a number of unhappy people. There would be people who had concerns but had never had a chance to voice them, or, when they did, no one listened. Without the caring, calming influence of the Golden Retrievers, it would be a lot easier for disagreements and arguments to pop up about what to do and who should do what. And there would be a lot of quiet people who would have missed out and yet wished they could have been involved.

And without the *Beaver's* part, well, it would just be a mess! Few of the details would have been carried out. When the time came to start the fair, there would be equipment missing, not enough space or food, confusion about who went where, and so on. A lot of things would have been forgotten along the way, and a lot of people probably would have no idea what they were supposed to do or where they should go.

Each person has a particular thing they bring to the team. Often we have more than one part we can contribute. It is important that we teach our children how to recognize the contributions each person makes and help them value the differences everyone brings. If Lions and Beavers worked alone, the event would happen but the people might be unhappy. If Otters and Golden Retrievers worked alone, the people would be happy but the event might not happen.

For a complete, successful event, both the task and the people need to be accommodated. And that's why God gave us each something special to contribute. We are all part of the body. And every part, whether we are comfortable with how that part works or not, is important. Training our children in this area will help them to work well in their community, whatever that community may be—school, youth group, friends, work, or family.

A good, practical time to apply this teaching is when your children have personality conflicts and come up with complaints like "She's so bossy," or "He's always trying to be funny and just get attention," or "They're so boring, they just want to plan everything to death."

These comments come when your child is first beginning to recognize the different personality types, which is a golden opportunity to help your children see other personality types in a positive light.

Not Weak but Blessed

Although each personality type has areas of strength and other areas in which they aren't as strong, it would be a serious mistake to label areas in which we are not as strong "weaknesses." God gave us individual personalities and then began adding to each person extra strengths. To one person He gave an ability to lead; to another one an extra zeal for life and having fun; to another one He gave an especially loving, caring heart; and to another a love of details and getting the little things right.

So what if the person with the ability to lead, our friend the Lion, does not have the love of details that the Beaver does? The Lion is not weak in that area but, rather, has the basic level of detail love that everyone gets. The Golden Retriever, with a caring heart, doesn't have the love of leading and forging ahead that the Lion does. It's not a weakness; it's just that the Golden Retriever has the ordinary amount of leading. And it's the same with all the personality type strengths. God doesn't give us weaknesses; He gives us strengths.

If your child is strong in *Influencing* like our friend the Otter, his or her weakest area may be in taking care of the details. This should not become an excuse: "That's not my personality type. I'm just not good at the details. That's not what I bring to the group."

If your children have this attitude, it'll probably carry over into their personal lives. They would never get organized, clean their rooms, learn how to handle money wisely, or take care of the little things and might use their personality type as an excuse. But this is not right!

When God gave your child the strengths of an *Influencing* person, He did not give him or her the weaknesses that preclude that child from having the abilities that a *Conscientious, Dominant,* or *Steady* person has. These are simply areas in which he or she has the normal, baseline abilities and can train and grow in these other areas.

We need to encourage our children not only to know what their strengths are and what they can best bring to a group but to grow in all these other zones in their own personal lives. God left us "neutral" in these other areas so that we could grow in them and so that we could be appreciative of others' strengths. When our children develop these other abilities, they have even more to bring to a group and can be more flexible.

God could have left us all on the baseline plateau without adding any extra strengths to us. Then we would have had to learn *all* the skills of the various personality types. Instead, He gifted us in some areas and gave us a head start so that we could function better in a group. And, since we are all a mixture of the personality types (none of us is purely a *Dominant* person or purely a *Steady* person), we have some of the "extras" for more than one of the personality types. It's an awesome blessing, but it should not reflect on who we are or mean that we can't have weaknesses in certain areas.

Once again, personality types are not an excuse for bad character or for laziness. We must be willing to work and strengthen the areas that are not as easy for us and don't come as naturally.

That's why we can't pigeonhole Jesus Christ as being one personality type or another. He was completely balanced and showed the strengths of all the personality types. And that should be our goal for ourselves and for our children.

Relating to Our Children's Types

Personality types are also a benefit to us as parents. When we understand our children's strengths and what they bring to a group, including the family, we can figure out more easily how to communicate and relate to them more effectively. These community strengths can be a great help to us as we try to teach our children the whole gamut of things they need to know in order to be fully equipped for life.

For example, if your daughter is a *Conscientious* person, good at being concerned with and taking care of details, you know that to communicate with her on this level will give you the greatest possibility of success. If she's concerned about something—say, a monster under her bed or fear of the dark—you can see the best way to alleviate her fears. First, you would explain that God is with her and looking after her; He didn't give us a spirit of fear. Then you would talk to her logically about her fear and say, "Look, there's nothing under your bed or in the closet when the light is on. Nothing can get into the room. So there's nothing there when the light is off either." Dealing with this logically, detail by detail, works for her because that's how she understands things.

If your *Influencing* son is afraid of the dark, the best way to help him is to tell him that he's safe and that you are nearby, right down the hallway. Being a people person, he needs to know that you are within call. Having the radio on or being able to hear voices in the kitchen assures him he's safe.

For your *Dominant* daughter, perhaps the best way is to let her figure it out but lead her through the solution. You will not easily talk her out of her fear, so you should let her work her own way around it. Ask her, "What could I do to make you feel safe? What would make you feel better?" Let her lead the way and find out for herself, hands-on. If she comes up with a solution, such as leaving a light on or having a hall light on and her bedroom door open, go with it. Once she suggests the solution, it will probably work for her.

If your son is a *Golden Retriever,* it's probably best to let him know that you love him and you're taking care of him. You understand how he feels, because you've felt that way yourself at times. Tell him what you did to deal with your fear of the dark. Assure him that even if there were monsters you'd never put him in harm's way. He needs to be assured that he is cared for, is loved, and is safe.

From this it should be clear how understanding our children's personality types can help us as we teach and guide them through life. When we learn to work in conjunction with their personality strengths, we make it easier for our children to learn.

Just as personality types can be used as a good way to understand how to communicate and train our children, those personality strengths will always be a dominant personality strength for them. Yes, they can develop the others, but God gives specific gifts for use in a community setting. This will always be a part of them and they will always have those tendencies.

When God gave them their personality types, He designed them perfectly, keeping in mind who they are, what their gifts and talents are, and what their genetic code is. He made sure that everything lined up perfectly; therefore, their personality types will become seeds of destiny for their lives and careers.

Some jobs seem ideally suited for certain personality types. For example, *Influencing* people often make ideal salespeople. They love to chat over coffee with people, spend time with various people, and motivate and convince others to try new and exciting things. Other personality types can be good salespeople also, when they learn to use their strengths effectively, but it seems to come more naturally to *Influencing* people.

Conscientious people often make good accountants; they fit well in jobs and professions in which the details are important.

Our children's personality types don't point to specific jobs or professions, but understanding the types can serve as signposts that point in a more general direction. We must help our kids keep their focus on

God and trust in Him to guide them to the goal He has in mind for them.

God is consistent. He designed us, gave us unique and wonderful spirits that match our DNAs and who we were when we were created from our parents. He specifically gave us personality types that will match us to the callings He gave us. So when we start to see a consistency in how God has made us, it gives us signposts to our children's calling. If we are reading the signposts properly and our children are growing in relationship with God, all the signposts will eventually start pointing in the right direction.[2]

Notes

1. For a more detailed look at personality types for children, see John Trent and Gary Smalley, *The Treasure Tree* (Word) and *The Two Trails* (Tommy Nelson).

2. The DISC system of personality types is laid out in great detail in *Your Career In Changing Times* and *Finding the Career That Fits You* by Lee Ellis and Larry Burkett (Moody Press).

1. Follow the instructions for the personality tests for you and your children in the Appendix. When you are finished, write your conclusions on a piece of paper and discuss the results. How did the results meet or differ from your expectations? Why do you think this is so?

2. Now that you are armed with this new information about your children, discuss their strengths with them in detail. How can they use them to be more effective in their tasks and relationships? What new activities should they consider in light of their strengths?

3. In terms of your children's tasks and activities, how do they see their strengths fitting in with those with whom they interact at home, at school, at church, or at other activities? How can they contribute to people who have strengths in other areas?

4. As your children begin to understand the four basic personality types, choose some people they interact with in a significant way who show strengths in different areas. Help them to identify those strengths and commit to work better with these people, to truly value their personalities.

5. Be sure to carefully explain the limitations of these personality tests with your child: The tests don't completely define us, they don't limit us, and they aren't exact. Get feedback to make sure your children put the tests in this perspective.

6. Because these tests don't limit us, we can grow in the areas that are not our strengths. Together with your child, pick the two weakest zones in his or her life, and come up with a plan for how your child can grow in these areas.

7. Now that you have learned much more about your children's personalities, how can you provide better wisdom, guidance, and discipline in your everyday communication with them?

Chapter 4

CHARACTER AND PERSONAL GROWTH

T he word *character* has been around for several thousand years. Over the centuries it has acquired quite a number of different meanings, especially in English. For example, the letters on this page are *characters*; Bugs Bunny is a cartoon *character*; actors play *characters* in movies. We all know people who are *real characters*—whose quirky personality traits make them just a bit different from the rest of us.

But there's a vast difference between *being a character* and *having character*. When we talk about people who *have* character, we mean they have certain qualities we admire, such as honesty, loyalty, a sense of duty, integrity, and so on. People who have bad character lack positive moral qualities and may be mean, underhanded, undependable, and so forth. The question is, by what standard do we determine what is good character and what is bad character?

Our society sees character as something that is socially determined. In other words, good character is the kind of character that best reflects the values and stability of society. For example, in a society that accepts blood feuds as a good and necessary thing, a man with character would be the one who would assume the responsibility to avenge the family's honor by killing a member of another family who had insulted his family.

In our own society, we don't reject greed as lack of character. Rather, greed is considered good because it stimulates the economy—never mind that people get hurt in the process.

In fact, we very often value success and celebrity status far more than we value character. We tend to admire the rich and famous, regardless of their character or lack thereof. We envy them, without really being concerned about how they amassed their wealth or became famous—whether honestly, immorally, or "by hook or by (mostly) crook."

In the Bible, the Greek word *character* is used once, in Hebrews 1:3: *"The Son* [Jesus] *is the radiance of God's glory and the* **exact representation** [character] *of his being"* (emphasis added).

This is close to the original meaning of the word, which came from a verb that meant to engrave (a meaning still reflected in calling a letter on the printed page a *character*—in the olden days, letters for a printing press were engraved in metal).

When God created us He created us according to His character. Jesus is the "character" of God; who He was and is shows us what God is like. And it is in this sense that we should understand and use the word character when talking about people.

True character is not determined by the changing values of society; it is measured by the absolute standard of who God is and what He's like. *True character is the assimilation and expression of God-likeness,* the living out of the traits that God possesses as part of His character, of who He is.

Character is solid and stable. Circumstances do not dictate it. There can be no "situational ethics" with true character, because godly character is the same, no matter what the situation is.

"And God saw that it was good" (Genesis 1:10, 12, 18, 21, 25). God said this about everything He created, but after He created mankind *"God saw all that he had made, and it was* **very** *good"* (Genesis 1:31 emphasis added). Then came the Fall, and the image of God was marred. Sin entered the world.

Jesus said, *"No one is good—except God alone"* (Mark 10:18). But the good news is that when we are born again God's Spirit enables us once again to grow in God-likeness. This is what character is.

Character never changes. It is the same, regardless of your personality. It matters not whether you are an extrovert who could sell an Apple computer to Bill Gates or a quiet, reticent person with a subtle dry wit and a love for art. Character lies at the very core of who you are, and it expresses itself through the filter of your personality in your behavior.

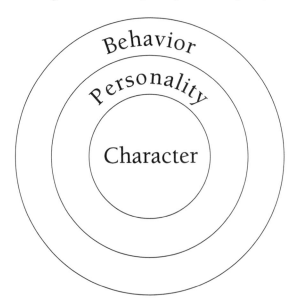

An analogy would be a computer. Let's say your child is the hardware—the computer itself. His or her personality, talents, and so forth are the software. Character is God's operating system. The operating system is what makes the computer run as it is designed. The most expensive and advanced software will produce nothing worthwhile without a fully functional operating system.

Character is what allows us to "fly through any weather," using God's "instruments." It is the rudder that enables us to go in whatever direction God wants us to go.

Character is constant, but it expresses itself differently in each one of us, for two reasons. First, we're all at different places in our growth. Some of us have certain character traits deeply ingrained in us (in other words, we've nailed them), but others of us are working hard to give that same character a toehold in our lives. However, we are all going to the same place and are on the same track; we're just at different places along the journey. Where we're going is defined by who God is. Where we are along this track defines to a certain extent what our character is.

The second reason our characters seem different has to do with how we express ourselves. We express honesty, integrity, or generosity through our personalities. Since my personality is different from yours, these traits will take a different form in my life than they do in yours. We might both be generous, but how we show our generosity differs because of who we are.

Character or Genes?

Before we look more closely at God's character and how we can teach our children to become more godlike in *their* character, we must briefly go back to the question of genetics. Our society has no consistent, objective concept of character; in fact, there is a tendency to see behavior (and by implication also character) as genetically determined.

We all remember from our high school science class that eye and hair color, body shape, and a few other things are determined by heredity— by our genes. Blue eyes are recessive, brown eyes are dominant. In Asia, black hair is prominent; but in Scandinavia, blond genes run rampant.

The question of heredity used to be fairly simple. You could even draw a chart with an *O* or an *X* to determine with some degree of accuracy what the chances were that a child would inherit a particular trait, such as blue eyes or premature baldness, from his or her parents.

But times have changed. Heredity has given way to genetics. Most people know that our genes contain DNA—long, intertwined molecules that are unique for each individual. A DNA molecule carries all the information necessary for the development of a person from a single fertilized egg cell to a fully grown adult. And it is supposed to do a whole lot more than determine the color of eyes and hair or the length of noses.

Do our genes determine us to such an extent that it doesn't make a whole lot of sense to talk about developing character and growing in godlikeness? Molecular biologists are searching for specific bits of DNA that may contribute to particular behaviors. The big question is, Are we born a certain way behaviorally? And if we are, does that mean we are not responsible for our actions? Can a legal defense be, "My genes made me do it"? And can that also be our excuse for not taking God's Word seriously when it talks about living and behaving in certain ways: "Sorry, God, it's in my genes—the ones You gave me"?

Recently, molecular biologist Dean Hamer created an enormous furor in the press, somewhat similar to the excitement over Dolly C. Sheep. He reported that he had found a common gene on the X chromosome of homosexual males. Soon headlines screamed "Gay Gene," "Made to Be Homosexual," and "Born Gay." Gay men were off the hook for any responsibility for a gay lifestyle: they had no choice. It also was said that Dr. Hamer had found a violence gene and a risk-taking gene.

But what many articles didn't mention is that the science of behavioral genetics is still in its infancy. We're still largely groping in the dark. To a significant degree, scientists are "guessing." In fact, Dr. Hamer himself emphasized that genes do not make people shy, homosexual, daredevils, or worriers. In spite of the media hype about the "gay gene," he asserts that there is no such thing. There's far more to the biology of personality than that.

It is also significant that no one has been able to reproduce Hamer's findings, which means that the links he found might not even exist. And the "genius gene," discovered by Dr. Robert Plomin of London's Institute of Psychiatry, is found also in people who are definitely not geniuses but not in a number of people who do fall in the genius category.[1]

In addition, looking for specific genes that influence particular behaviors is like looking for a needle in a field of haystacks.[2] Even if the needle is found, we have to keep in mind how genes actually work. They're not like light switches that, when flicked to "on" in an individual, make that person gay or violent or happy or sad.

What precisely do the DNA molecules of your genes do? Do they produce thoughts? No. Can they cause emotions? No. Do they determine behavior? No. Genes do not make you react a certain way. They do not control how you behave.

The purpose of genes is simply to produce proteins. The function of proteins is to act as enzymes and change one chemical into another.

These chemicals affect the brain, and although they can create a tendency toward certain responses scientists theorize that it probably takes an untold number of different proteins working together to create a predisposition toward a specific temperament.

All genes, neurotransmitters, and hormones do is influence how you tend to respond. You might have a genetic predisposition in a certain direction—such as a short temper—but how you actually respond to any given situation is entirely a matter of free will, guided by conscience and character.

God has made us in accordance with who He is, and as our children grow toward His character, any genetic vulnerabilities, tendencies, predispositions will be used by God for our children's growth and to the glory of Him who *"works for the good of those who love him"* (Romans 8:28).

It's always risky to draw absolute conclusions based on the current state of affairs. What if someone born with a genius gene, a patience gene, a funding gene, and a lucky gene manages to prove that there really are such things as an anxiety gene, a gay gene, and a genius gene? In other words, what if science were to prove at some point in the future that our behavior is to a large extent genetically determined? It would change nothing.

We know that God is good. Even if through sin our genetic heritage has been marred, we know that *"If anyone is in Christ, he is a new creation; the old has gone, the new has come!"* (2 Corinthians 5:17). Yes, God holds us accountable for our actions: *"A man reaps what he sows"* (Galatians 6:7), but God seems to think that we can follow Him, regardless of our natural tendencies. That is why He gave us His Holy Spirit: *"When he, the Spirit of truth, comes, he will guide you into all truth"* (John 16:13). It is the Spirit of God who will guide us in the truth of God's character, into becoming God-like in character.

The Holy Spirit has the ability to change us, and that is something that transcends science. The Holy Spirit can never be found by scientific research. Jesus said when He talked with Nicodemus: *"The wind blows wherever it pleases. You hear its sound, but you cannot tell where it comes from or where it is going. So it is with everyone born of the Spirit"* (John 3:8).

The work of the Spirit is not part of our finite, three-dimensional world in which we observe cause and effect. All we can see of the Spirit's work is the results: transformed lives and characters molded into the likeness of God's character.

Teaching Character

God's character is who He is. He does not change. If He is loving, He is *always* loving. God's character is the bedrock of what He is like: as solid and unchangeable as God Himself. *"I the Lord **do not change"*** (Malachi 3:6 emphasis added). *"Every good and perfect gift is from above, coming down from the Father of the heavenly lights, **who does not change like shifting shadows"*** (James 1:17 emphasis added).

Furthermore, God created us so that we could have the character traits He has. (At the end of this chapter you'll find the seven main character traits of God, with verses showing that the traits belong to God, as well as a motto and memory verse for each.)

The key is to get our children's "software" (returning to my computer analogy) to mesh with this character-operating system. To do that we need to try to instill in them each of these main character traits.

So, for example, we teach our children that there is *never* a reason to lie. We never lie, no matter what. It's as simple as that. God is honest and wants us to be honest. What's more, being honest works best. Explain to them why this is so: God made the world to work this way. When we're honest, people trust us and want to be friends. We get a reputation for being people who always tell it straight.

In contrast, if we don't tell the truth, things start to fall apart. People find out about it and stop trusting us, because they can't believe us anymore. Most people don't want to be friends with people who lie to them. Why would they?

We teach our children that they can *choose* to tell the truth. They need to *decide* that they're going to be like God. They need to decide that they are going to install this operating system into their computers to operate all their software. When it's been installed, they'll be determined that, no matter what their individual personalities are like, what their talents are, what they're called to do, what experiences they have, or what situations they find themselves in, they will purposefully not be dishonest—because honesty is a part of their character. They will say with conviction, "I'm truthful and honest."

Your children should be taught to be people of strong character. Teach them the character traits God wants us all to have and help them *choose* those character traits. You want your children to be able to affirm the character traits as being their own—not only who they want to be but who they *are*. Show them that the Bible tells us to be this way; then give them verses, such as the verses above, that support this.

Children need to learn these things and hold them with confidence. They need to understand that when they have this kind of character, they fit in with how God made them and everything else to work. Be sure your children understand that if they want great, happy, fulfilled lives, then they will need to live according to how their lives were designed. It's only logical.

Trying to run computers with defective operating systems just doesn't make sense. In fact, it will lead to some very frustrating and costly crashes. If we want to get the best out of our computers, we learn to install the operating systems and use them to the fullest capabilities.

It's the same with character. If we try to live and run our lives against God's operating system, sooner or later we will crash. But using it well will give us a smoothly running life that will bring results we can't even imagine, because everything is working in harmony. *"Continue to work out your salvation with fear and trembling, for it is God who works in you to will and to act according to his good purpose"* (Philippians 2:12–13).

Expressing and Developing Character

Almost without thinking about it, we teach our kids other principles for happy lives. For example, we teach them to look both ways before crossing the street, and we don't allow them a choice in the matter. We clearly explain it to them and walk them through the process, making sure they understand the urgency of the situation. In the same way, we should teach them about character and the various character traits. These are the pillars on which their day-to-day lives will depend. They are as basic to lifesaving as "look both ways before you cross the street."

So how do you help your children grow in character? The most important thing to teach them is that it is a matter of choice: *choose* God's way. Also, explain that they will be growing in character their whole lives; teach them the *attitude of growth.* Every single day they need to choose to grow, to look to God and His character, and to become more like Him.

It's important that we don't just teach our children to *do* the right thing. That's not character. D.L. Moody said, "Character is what you are in the dark." Character is who you *are,* not what you *do.* It's not just that I'm going to *do* what's right. I'm going to *be* right.

The Pharisees did what was right, externally. But that wasn't enough. Inside they were full of death. The doing must spring from the being. God is love, and His loving actions come out of His being love. These pillars of character need to become essential parts of who our children are. When the opportunity comes to lie, they simply will choose not to lie, because they know they are honest.

An easy, but important, teaching tip is this: Begin identifying your children with these character traits. You shouldn't say, "Well, Johnny just has trouble sharing." Rather, say, "Johnny is learning to be generous." When Johnny wants to hide behind the fact that he's a certain way, for example, by saying, "I just can't share right now," it's important not to let that go. Help Johnny identify with who he is, as a generous person. Say something like, "Yes, you can. You're a person who shares with others. Remember when you shared. . . ." Give an example of a time when he did share and remind him of how good it felt and how well it worked out. Reinforce the times he has shared. Help Johnny identify with generosity—that's who he is.

Conversely, don't tell your children they are bad. Instead, take the stance that they *did* something bad but that they *are* developing godly character. Then you can use the opportunity to teach them about the correct response so that, next time, they can do it God's way.

Vessels of Honor

God loves us, and He designed us in a special way that goes perfect-ly with His direction for us—His awesome plan. We can all walk in God's fullness, but to do that we need to grow in character. God won't take our children where He wants them to go unless they're growing in character—because it won't work. In order to be in places where they can serve others, work in God's kingdom, and help people, they need to have godly character. It's the same principle as not letting an eight-year-old drive a car. The child just isn't ready for it!

"In a large house there are articles not only of gold and silver, but also of wood and clay; some are for noble purposes and some for ignoble. If a man cleanses himself from the latter, he will be an instrument for noble purposes, made holy, useful to the Master and prepared to do any good work" (2 Timothy 2:20–21).

Let's cleanse ourselves and be vessels fit for noble purposes; and let's teach our children to do the same. The more they grow in character, cleanse themselves from sinful things, identify with God, and do things God's way, the more they'll change. The more they're faithful in changing, the more God can trust them and the further He can take them into His plan. They'll become useful to the Master and ready to do the good works He's prepared ahead of time for them to do. *"We are God's workmanship, created in Christ Jesus to do good works, which God prepared in advance for us to do"* (Ephesians 2:10).

It's impossible to move forward in God's individual plan for your children without them knowing who God has called them to be. Character comes before the plan. That doesn't mean that they have to be perfect before they can fit into God's plan, but as they grow in character God will move them along in His plan. Growth in character and growth in the other areas of their lives should go hand in hand.

Even though God has an awesome plan for your children, if you try to move them ahead in His plan, although they haven't grown in character and haven't submitted their lives to Him, it will destroy not only them but also the people they would be leading and affecting. And they would become vessels of dishonor, vessels for ignoble purposes.

The Prodigal Son became a vessel of dishonor. He became a vessel to teach us how things don't work—*how not to do it*. He was selfish and greedy, ignored character, and just went for pleasure—short-term pleasure. However, when he repented and turned his life around, his father accepted him back into the family. As he grew, he became a vessel of honor, suitable for noble purposes. Help your children to be vessels ready to be used for noble purposes, useful to the Master.

Seven Traits of God's Character

In teaching children to develop character, it's helpful to show them the model: God's character. Below are seven traits of God's character, with Bible verses to show that these traits really are part of who God is.

Since children need the affirmation that they are like God, we have included a motto with each trait that you can teach your children. The motto helps them decide if they have that character trait. Also included are some memory verses that show that God wants us to have that character. When they learn the memory verses, they will always have the reminder with them in times of decision.

1. God Is True and Honest

"*Into your hands I commit my spirit; redeem me, O Lord, the God of truth*" (Psalm 31:5).

"*This is eternal life: that they may know you, the only true God, and Jesus Christ, whom you have sent*" (John 17:3).

"*God did this so that, by two unchangeable things in which it is impossible for God to lie, we. . . take hold of the hope offered to us*" (Hebrews 6:18).

"*We know also that the Son of God has come and has given us understanding, so that we may know him who is true. And we are in him who is true—even in his Son Jesus Christ. He is the true God and eternal life*" (1 John 5:20).

Motto: "I'm truthful and honest like God."

I will always tell the truth, even when it's hard. I'll be honest with everyone I meet. And I'll make sure the way I tell the truth is kind and loving.

Memory verses

"*Whatever is true, whatever is noble, whatever is right, whatever is pure, whatever is lovely, whatever is admirable—if anything is excellent or praiseworthy—think about such things*" (Philippians 4:8).

"*Speaking the truth in love, we will in all things grow up into him who is the Head, that is, Christ*" (Ephesians 4:15).

2. God Is Loving and Compassionate

"He passed in front of Moses, proclaiming, 'The Lord, the Lord, the compassionate and gracious God, slow to anger, abounding in love and faithfulness'" (Exodus 34:6).

"Give thanks to the God of gods. His love endures forever" (Psalm 136:2).

"God is love" (1 John 4:8).

Motto: "God is loving and compassionate and so am I."

I will love people and treat them gently. I will be compassionate toward everyone I meet. If I make a mistake, I'll seek forgiveness and then go on working love into my life. Whether I'm a singer or an engineer is irrelevant to my character. Whatever I do, I'll do it in a loving, compassionate way.

Memory verses

"This is my command: Love each other" (John 15:17).

"Therefore, as God's chosen people, holy and dearly loved, clothe yourselves with compassion, kindness, humility, gentleness and patience" (Colossians 3:12).

3. God Is Generous and Selfless

"'Test me in this,' says the Lord Almighty, 'and see if I will not throw open the floodgates of heaven and pour out so much blessing that you will not have room enough for it'" (Malachi 3:10).

"Give, and it will be given to you. A good measure, pressed down, shaken together and running over, will be poured into your lap" (Luke 6:38).

"He who did not spare his own Son, but gave him up for us all—how will he not also, along with him, graciously give us all things?" (Romans 8:32).

"Every good and perfect gift is from above, coming down from the Father of the heavenly lights, who does not change like shifting shadows" (James 1:17).

Motto: "I am generous and selfless, as God is."

I'm going to serve others in my community. I'm going to be generous and give. I'll look to the needs of others and not just to my own.

Memory Verse
"Command them to do good, to be rich in good deeds, and to be generous and willing to share" (1 Timothy 6:18).

4. God Is Forgiving and Merciful

"Praise the Lord, O my soul, and forget not all his benefits—who forgives all your sins and heals all your diseases" (Psalm 103:2–3).

"The Lord our God is merciful and forgiving, even though we have rebelled against him" (Daniel 9:9).

"Who is a God like you, who pardons sin and forgives the transgression of the remnant of his inheritance? You do not stay angry forever but delight to show mercy" (Micah 7:18).

Motto: "I am forgiving and merciful."

It's part of my character so, whatever happens, however people treat me, I will forgive. When people want something from me that they don't deserve, I'll be merciful and give it to them; I'll go the second mile for them.

Memory Verse
"Bear with each other and forgive whatever grievances you may have against one another. Forgive as the Lord forgave you" (Colossians 3:13).

5. God Is Trustworthy and Faithful

"Know therefore that the Lord your God is God; he is the faithful God, keeping his covenant of love to a thousand generations of those who love him and keep his commands" (Deuteronomy 7:9).

"O Sovereign Lord, you are God! Your words are trustworthy, and you have promised these good things to your servant" (2 Samuel 7:28).

"The law of the Lord is perfect, reviving the soul. The statutes of the Lord are trustworthy, making wise the simple" (Psalm 19:7).

"God, who has called you into fellowship with his Son Jesus Christ our Lord, is faithful" (1 Corinthians 1:9).

Motto: "I'm trustworthy and faithful."

Anyone who knows me will be able to trust me. I'll always do something kind. I'll do the right thing. I'll never do anything to hurt people intentionally. If I say I'm going to do something, I will. I'm faithful. I keep my word. That's what God is like and that's what I'm like.

<u>Memory Verses</u>
"But the fruit of the Spirit is love, joy, peace, patience, kindness, goodness, faithfulness, gentleness and self-control. Against such things there is no law" (Galatians 5:22–23).

"This calls for patient endurance on the part of the saints who obey God's commandments and remain faithful to Jesus" (Revelation 14:12).

6. God Is Just and Impartial

"He is the Rock, his works are perfect, and all his ways are just. A faithful God who does no wrong, upright and just is he" (Deuteronomy 32:4).

"God is just" (2 Thessalonians 1:6).

"The wisdom that comes from heaven is first of all pure; then peace-loving, considerate, submissive, full of mercy and good fruit, impartial and sincere" (James 3:17).

"Salvation and glory and power belong to our God, for true and just are his judgments" (Revelation 19:1–2).

<u>**Motto: "I'm just and impartial."**</u>
When I'm making decisions, I won't show favoritism. I'm fair with everyone, no matter who they are. I'll always hear both sides of a story. I won't treat people differently because they're popular, or cool, or have money, or because they're different than I am. I treat everyone the same. I will love what is good and hate what is evil.

<u>Memory Verses</u>
"You have neglected the more important matters of the law—justice, mercy and faithfulness. You should have practiced the latter, without neglecting the former" (Matthew 23:23).

"Love does not delight in evil but rejoices with the truth" (1 Corinthians 13:6).

"But the wisdom that comes from heaven is first of all pure; then peace-loving, considerate, submissive, full of mercy and good fruit, impartial and sincere" (James 3:17).

7. *God Is Holy*

"*You are to be holy to me because I, the Lord, am holy*" (Leviticus 20:26).

"*There is no one holy like the Lord*" (1 Samuel 2:2).

"*Holy, holy, holy is the Lord God Almighty, who was, and is, and is to come*" (Revelation 4:8).

Motto: "I'm growing toward being holy like God."

I'm going to keep myself from the sins of the world. I'm going to avoid things that are impure—that are not like God. I won't speak in an impure way or get involved in sinful things. That is my character and that doesn't change. If I make a mistake, I'll ask God to forgive me and help me be pure.

Memory Verses

"*Therefore, I urge you, brothers, in view of God's mercy, to offer your bodies as living sacrifices, holy and pleasing to God—this is your spiritual act of worship*" (Romans 12:1).

"*God did not call us to be impure, but to live a holy life*" (1 Thessalonians 4:7).

Notes

1. *Newsweek*, May 25, 1998.
2. A *Time* article that explored the issue of personality genes (April 27, 1998) reminds us that DNA is made of four chemicals. A single human gene may be made up of as many as a million combinations of these chemicals! In addition, most genes vary between individuals only by one chemical letter in a thousand. These tiny differences are what behavioral geneticists like Hamer are looking for. Yet, the sensationalistic media coverage of Hamer's discoveries made it appear that science had proven once for all that homosexuality was genetic. As was, they said, violence.

1. Think up some ways to show your children how different cultures have different character standards. Then show them how God alone defines character. Ask your child how he or she might explain the difference between some of society's values and God's standards.

2. Take an opportunity to discover what your child really understands about Jesus by asking him or her which qualities in Jesus' life reflect the character of God and how He used them in His life on earth.

3. How do you see character and personality working together in your child's life? For example, how is honesty displayed in a way that is peculiar to his or her personality type? Ask yourself the same question about other character qualities.

4. Much of society has the "victim" mentality—the view that wrong behavior is determined by upbringing or genes. Test your child's understanding of our accountability before God and how the Spirit transforms us.

5. Choose two of God's character traits that your child may have trouble understanding. Have him or her do further Bible study on these areas and work on the memory verses. Then let your child share with you what he or she has learned.

6. Review the teaching pattern on honesty found in the section on how to teach character. Together with your child, apply this logical pattern of thought to other character traits.

7. God can only use people of character for His purposes. Explain the phrase "vessels of honor" by using examples of talented people who repented of their sin (such as John Newton) and only then were used by God.

Part 2

CALLING

"When I was woven together in the depths of the earth, your eyes saw my unformed body. All the days ordained for me were written in your book before one of them came to be"
(Psalm 139:15–16).

Chapter 5

DESTINY
AND CALLING

Zushya, a Jewish rabbi who lived in the Ukraine at the end of the eighteenth century, is remembered mostly for one statement. He said, "In the world to come, I will not be asked, 'Why weren't you Moses?' I will be asked, 'Why weren't you Zushya?'"

He understood a profound truth. God made each one of us to be uniquely ourselves. He gave us genetic endowments that He matched perfectly with our spirits. He gave us talents. And He had a unique plan.

David said, *"I praise you because I am fearfully and wonderfully made; your works are wonderful, I know that full well. My frame was not hidden from you when I was made in the secret place. When I was woven together in the depths of the earth, your eyes saw my unformed body. All the days ordained for me were written in your book before one of them came to be"* (Psalm 139:14–16).

God did not give us personality, talents, and the ability to grow in character, only to leave us to fend for ourselves. He planned ahead for us, as we just read in the Scripture verse above: *"All the days ordained for me were written in your book before one of them came to be."*

When our children stand before God our Father in eternity, one of the most wonderful things God could say to them is, "You trusted Me and let Me make you into the person I created you to be. You were the person whose personality, talents, and gifts I lovingly put together and carefully crafted. You fulfilled My plan for you."

You see, God matches who we *are* to what we *do* with our lives. As our Father, he knows and understands us and our children completely. He has planned how we fit into His overall plan for His creation, and He is willing and able to help all of us execute that plan. Fulfilling God's plan for our lives doesn't happen automatically; yet, we don't have to strenuously try to find God's plan for our lives, always afraid that we might miss it.

What God asks is that we come to Him in faith, willing to be led by Him, and then trust Him to guide us in the practical things of everyday life, both large and small, while we do the work He has given us to the best of our ability.

What's in a Job?

In this and the following chapters, we'll talk about the actual process your children can go through to find and follow God's plan for their lives. Looking around us, it would seem that finding the place where one fits into the world of work (the world where most of us will spend more than half of our adult waking hours) eludes many, many people—including many Christians.

A bit more comprehensive information comes from a Hewitt Associates survey of 46,500 employees from 38 different companies. One in four (27 percent) reported being dissatisfied with their jobs, and half of the workers (50 percent) reported being dissatisfied with the recognition they received at work.[1]

A Gallup Poll asked people whether they would continue to work at their present jobs if they won the lottery. Approximately two out of three said they would not.[2]

The Associates for Research Into the Science of Enjoyment (ARISE) recently published the results of an international survey on job stress. Over half of office workers say that work is the main cause of stress in their lives. Every fifth office worker admitted that he or she had taken time off work due to stress. And it doesn't seem to matter where the worker is in the company's hierarchy: senior directors, CEOs, middle managers, and secretaries make this admission in the same proportions.[3]

The same survey discovered that the level of job dissatisfaction also was evenly spread through the ranks—about one in four people in high management admit that, given the opportunity, they would not choose the same line of work again.

It seems clear that a lot of people are not where they want to be or where they belong, as far as work and careers go. A lot of people in the workforce are not doing their jobs because they love them or want to do them but because they have jobs in which they can make money. If people were doing what they were suited and designed for, they would be enjoying their work; they would find it stimulating and fulfilling. How have so many people made mistakes in their lifework choice?

Seven Career Motivators

Job dissatisfaction has a number of causes, but one of them lies in the reasons why people choose their careers in the first place. Traditionally, many people choose careers because their parents, directly or indirectly, motivated them to move in a certain direction.

It's helpful to look at the motivators that parents have used over the years and how these motivators have changed as our society has changed. You'll probably recognize all of them. Note the progression as we go.

1. Follow Me

In the past, a particular craft, occupation, or business tended to stay in a family. Parents encouraged their children to follow in their footsteps and take over the family businesses, which was easy and made sense. A father wanted this because he was proud of what he had accomplished. He wanted his legacy to grow and expand as it stayed in the family as a kind of monument to his and his family's success.

For example, a man says to his son, "Your grandfather ran this butcher shop. I've run this butcher shop. And you're going to run this butcher shop. Come in here and I'll show you how to cut this meat. I'll teach you how to find the best cuts and how to mind the store."

The son turns away from his dream of being a carpenter and sighs, "I'm coming, Dad."

This example points out the problem with this motivator: The child might have no interest whatsoever in being a butcher. He might get sick at the sight of blood, be a lousy businessperson, or dream of a career that would include working out of doors or perhaps traveling. For him, the struggle to take over the family business would lead to frustration, regret, and perhaps eventually bankruptcy.

Trying to push our children toward careers we are in might meet our needs as parents, but it doesn't necessarily meet our children's needs. Nor does it consider God's plan for that child.

John Smoltz is the 1996 winner of the Cy Young award, the highest award for pitchers in the baseball league in the United States. He also was voted the most valuable player in baseball in the U.S.

John's parents wanted him to become a musician, because they were both musicians. But once they discovered his love of baseball, they abandoned their own ambitions for him and helped him become the best baseball player he could be. John's dad spent hundreds of hours practicing baseball with John, even though he knew very little about it. Because of the dedication of John's parents, and especially his father, John became the number one baseball pitcher in the entire world and the Most Valuable Player in the world for baseball that year. His parents were wise enough to recognize John's interests and abilities and to focus on those, even though their own expectations were not realized.

John is a fine Christian, as are his parents. He speaks to kid's groups and has been an inspiration to a lot of kids. He always gives praise to the Lord, and he always praises his parents for being willing to help him be the best he could be, in spite of the fact that it wasn't what they would have chosen for him.

Most professional athletes who have achieved anything did so because their parents were dedicated to helping them. It requires a total focus on what they're doing, and they can't do this without their parents.

2. Do What I Never Did

Society has changed rapidly. During the Great Depression, jobs were limited. People did whatever was needed in order to survive.

Then, after the Depression and after the advances in technology brought about as a result of the war, the job market changed radically. Suddenly there were more choices available, with lots of options and opportunities. Parents started looking at their lives and seeing the opportunities they had missed, so they decided to work hard and save money to put their kids through college—to give their children the chance to do what they themselves had never had the chance to do.

Picture the father who says to his child, "Come on, let's play catch. You know, I could have been a professional ballplayer if I'd had the chance. Well, I'm going to make sure you have no regrets like that. You'll have the best arm in the league. I'll have you lifting weights when you're twelve, and you'll be the best there is."

But the child misses every ball the father throws. Finally the child says, "Dad, even if I get better, what if they won't let girls play in the league?"

"Do what I never did" wasn't, and still isn't, a good motivator, because it allows only who the parent is and what the parent desires. Unfortunately, or fortunately, your child is not the same as you. Your motive may be good; after all, you want the best for your child.

You want your children to have opportunities you never had; however, wanting them to accomplish something for you is a limited motivation. The key is to make sure that the something you want to give your children is what suits them as individuals and not your desire to shape copies of what you wanted to be. That motivator is as incomplete as the previous one. It still doesn't consider your children's individuality and unique design. Nor does it look at what God might have in mind for them.

3. Achievement

Society in the 60s and 70s went through a time of idealism. Being able to make a difference and help shape society became important. And so society began to push children toward a whole different range of careers, such as lawyer, doctor—even politician. Children were pushed toward that sort of intellectual achievement. The focus on achievement says, "This is what I think an honorable life is all about. This is what would have been cool if it had happened for me, if I'd achieved this, had gotten these honors, and had made this name for myself. You should do that. Be someone who will make a difference."

A mother says to her child, "You're going to be a neurosurgeon. They're respected and well thought of, partly because there are so few of them. I know you can do it because you have such great hand-eye coordination; your fine motor skills are incredible. And you're very intelligent; you learn quickly; you can pick up anything!"

"But, Mommy," the child replies plaintively, "I'm only four."

What you wish you had achieved might not be what your children want to achieve. It may not be what your children have talents and gifts for either. This motivator too is incomplete and skewed, taking into account the parents' desires more than the children's.

Over the decades there has been a progression from "follow me" to "do what I didn't" to "make me proud." This is an upwardly progressive path. Then, suddenly, we hit the "big bucks" motivator, which is greatly influenced by society's growing affluence.

4. Make Money

This brings us up to today. In the last couple of decades our society has become very materialistic and so have the motivations parents use to influence their children in choosing jobs. The belief is that the key to happiness is having lots of money. So now parents want their children to get jobs that will make the big bucks.

For the most part, big bucks aren't earned without an education. So, these days a college degree is almost a must. In 1987, only half of the students polled planned to attend college. In 1992, two out of three students planned to attend college full-time after high school graduation.[4]

A 1996 survey of all college freshmen in the United States showed that the four top occupations for males were engineer, business executive (management), computer programmer/analyst, and physician. Three of the top four occupations for females were physician, business executive (management), and nurse.[5]

Just over half of the teens surveyed by Gallup recently indicated that money was the most important consideration in having a successful career and life.[6]

One of the main reasons the occupations named are being chosen is because of what they pay. Many young people choose jobs that will give them the kind of money they want to have and then they pursue that job through education. This should not be surprising as we look around and consider our society's value system: the key to a happy life is big bucks. And so our children, who want to be happy, pursue what they believe will give them the big bucks.

Furthermore, our kids are surrounded by the news of how much money entertainers and sports professionals make. Young people look up to these "stars," want to have what they have, and are convinced that these people are on the top of the world. It follows that these societal heroes influence our children as they choose careers to pursue.

In fact, of the ten men most admired by teenagers in 1996, eight were professional athletes, musicians, or actors, and two were political leaders.[7] Of the ten women most admired by teenagers in 1997, eight were professional entertainers or models and the other two were involved in politics and social action.[8]

Our society is at a stage at which hope in the slow-but-steady, work-hard-to-get-ahead, be-content-where-you-are philosophies of life have lost ground. People see the good life slipping away because they believe earning big bucks is the only way to be happy, and most don't see how they can get it. The only real hope comes from the stories we watch in the news about those who strike it rich and get famous.

Society tells our youth to gain money, whether it's through education, becoming famous, or striking it rich; then they'll have it all and be happy. And so we have jobs such as engineers, business CEOs, and doctors topping the list for young people seeking higher education and everything from winning the lottery to becoming a rock star topping the list of many others. But easy come, easy go.

The truth is that only one in 100 professional athletes end their careers with any money to speak of, and many stars end up with nothing except enormous tax liabilities. And how many stories have we heard of wealthy rock stars being consumed by drugs or committing suicide? Money is not the answer. If it were, why would only one in six marriages of professional athletes survive their professional careers? To put it differently, why is the divorce rate of professional athletes five times the national average?

Until recently, there has been little or nothing in our society that tells youth to examine what they really want to do, what they're best suited for, what they believe in, what their values are, what they would like to do with their lives, and how they can contribute to their community—and then make decisions accordingly.

Going the next step and asking what God wants or has planned for them to do is not even considered in our society at large. Even we as Christian parents, wanting the best for our children, sometimes find ourselves pushing them toward the big bucks.

Sometimes this motivator comes out of the thought that money truly will make the child happy. Sometimes it's a desire for prestige on our part. We want our children to be rich and/or famous for the recognition of raising such great kids. Also, underneath this could be the desire to be well-looked-after in our old age. Either way, it's usually a wrong set of motivators. And, again, it is incomplete. For one thing, money is not a guarantee of happiness. For another, it does not consider your children's abilities, wants, or place in God's plan.

5. Be Spiritual

As Christians, we often have been on a slightly different trail. We've thought that in order to be a spiritual person we have to go into the full-time ministry. Somehow it seems a good reflection on our spirituality as parents and shows what a "good job" we've done when our children are serving the Lord "full-time."

This can lead to our children feeling guilty or feeling as if they should do this to please us, rather than finding what God wants them to do. But it could very well be that this is not what they're suited to or called to. We need to be careful that we're not trying to live our lives through our kids and motivate them with our ideas of what would be good and what would make us look or feel good.

A young girl walks in and asks, "Mom, how do you like my new nose ring?"

"Speaking of nose rings, dear," Mom replies, "I hear they're big in Africa. Have you thought any more about being a missionary? You could fit in really well there. I think God is preparing you to go to Africa. It's a very special calling."

"But, Mom," the daughter says in frustration, "I just wanted to know if you liked the nose ring!"

A so-called spiritual job is no more important than any other. We need to realize that God doesn't put any more significance on someone who is gifted or called to be a pastor than He does on someone who's a doctor, secretary, construction worker, or stay-at-home mom. We shouldn't think that our children need to be in full-time ministry to serve the Lord.

Again, the problem is that this is not the right set of motivations on our part. It's very limited. It doesn't consider the child. Nor does it consider that God's plan for the child might be quite different from ours. In fact, all these motivators fall short because they attempt to meet the parents' needs rather than the child's. None of them take into consideration what the child might want or be good at. And not considering these things has certainly contributed to the level of job dissatisfaction that pervades our society.

6. Do What You Want

As a reaction to the first five of these motivators that all neglected the child, a new movement with a new set of motivators is gaining ground. A motivator that is becoming popular these days focuses on our children's desires. We encourage them to look at what they want and then go for it. We have them ask themselves, "What would I really like to do?" They consider it and decide, for example, that they'd like to be a professional rock climber. That sounds fantastic: Fresh air. Exercise. Challenge. The beauty of nature all around. What a job! But they fail to consider that they're not athletic enough to be able to make a career of it—if a career can even be made of it.

They should stop to consider that something they desire right now is not necessarily what they will want in ten years. By that time they could be sick of it or just not want to do it anymore. There are lots of examples of people who choose college majors because they think it's what they want, and yet when they get the career they've studied for they discover it isn't what they wanted at all. Then we're left with yet another incomplete motivator.

7. Do What You're Good At

Being aware of the limits of simply trying to do what our children want, we have begun to look at what they would be good at. Many schools now administer personality and aptitude tests to their students to help them find out who they are, what they want to do, and what their talents or gifts are. We're starting to encourage our kids to give less importance to the money motivators (although money is still the biggest factor) and even the motivators that come out of what we as their parents want. Instead, we are encouraging them to search to find out who they are. The theory goes that knowing who they are and what their talents or gifts are will tell them unerringly what career will make them happy.

My (Rick's) brother Ryan was given a very extensive career aptitude test at the end of high school. It was a high-tech computerized test that considered a large number of factors, and the result showed that Ryan would be an excellent magician! To him, this was a completely undesired, impractical, and laughable result.

Once again (and why are we not surprised?) we've come a long way, but this motivator is still limited. The problem arises that when we find out what our gift or talent is a whole list of other things are not considered, such as what the job market is going to be like, what the future holds, and whether we're reading our talents correctly.

For example, you may do a career assessment with your daughter and discover that she would be a good veterinarian. So she thinks, "Wow! Veterinarians make pretty good money. I'm supposed to be good at that. I'll do it." Yet she has never explored the career, found out what a vet does, or even asked herself if this is what she wants to do with the rest of her life.

Pursuing a career from a motivation based primarily on talents and gifts does not guarantee success in placing ourselves in the right future and career.

Although career aptitude tests and looking at our desires can provide helpful indicators of what we may be good at, if we are motivated completely by our desires or completely by what we think our talents and gifts are, we still can be stumped and left in dead-end jobs that we hate.

God's Career Counseling

The truth is that *all* of these motivators are incomplete. Even if we try and consider all of the different ones and balance them out, we're still missing big pieces of the picture: We're missing the future. We're missing what changes will happen. Who could have predicted twenty years ago that computers would develop as quickly as they have, to say nothing of the Internet?

All of this brings us to the question, "Are there really right careers for our children?" We wonder if it matters what they choose and, if it does, how do they make the right choices?

There is only one complete, all-encompassing motivator that can guarantee career and job satisfaction: putting our lives into God's hands. He knows everything: past, present, and future. He also knows our kids completely. He created them, so He knows what they are best suited for, what they will enjoy and find fulfilling, and what will be the best thing for them. He is the ultimate career counselor!

With God, our children may still go through a variety of careers as the job market changes, but each one will suit them and prepare them for the next step. The satisfaction comes not in the career or the money, prestige, or fame it brings, but in doing what God has designed them to do and in fitting into God's plans, rather than just earning a living.

God has a calling, a career, a life in mind for our kids that is perfect for who they are. And He has given them the talents, gifts, and abilities they need to accomplish that plan. His planned direction for their lives includes giving them the opportunity to grow into who He's gifted them to be—not only in this life but for all of eternity. So He matches who He built them to be to His purpose for them, taking into account every day of their lives, including where they're going to fit into history, what they're going to do, and who they're going to be around.

When your sons and daughters ask God what His plan is for them and what He has for them to do, and then follow Him in that, He molds and shapes them, developing the talents He's given them. The result is that they fit right into what God has for them in this world. And they become someone who adds to our community, family, and world. They become people who make differences and are fulfilled.

Think of it this way. Let's say there's an intense, overnight mountain hike that you've made several times. You know how far apart the water holes are, so you know how much water you have to carry. And you understand that you need to budget your resources so that you'll be rested when you hit that really steep part. You know what you need to take along for the journey. When a friend wants to take that hike with you, knowing what's ahead, you will help that person get properly equipped for the journey.

God knew what was ahead of them when He so carefully "knit together" our children in their mothers' wombs. He made sure they would be properly equipped for their journeys, and He gave them everything they would need as a blessing. He made them specially fit for their particular "hike" through life. God knows the beginning from the end, and He has equipped them perfectly for the journey.

Relationship

Much time has been spent debating the question about what God knows, when and how He plans, and when and how our wills and responses are involved. There are two extremes on the theological spectrum in this debate. One side asserts that God controls everything: It's all preplanned and no input from us will make any difference.

The other side believes that God made everything but then left it up to us to decide what we would do. Fortunately, the discussion is moot. Nowhere in the Bible does it tell us to figure out how God does His job. In contrast, there are a number of verses that tell us that we will never figure Him out.

"'My thoughts are not your thoughts, neither are your ways my ways,' declares the Lord. 'As the heavens are higher than the earth, so are my ways higher than your ways and my thoughts than your thoughts'" (Isaiah 55:8–9).

"They do not know the thoughts of the Lord; they do not understand his plan, he who gathers them like sheaves to the threshing floor" (Micah 4:12).

"Now we see but a poor reflection as in a mirror. . . . Now I know in part" (1 Corinthians 13:12).

We won't and don't need to figure out how God does His job, but there is a key that helps us find and understand God's plan for our lives. The key is not in trying to figure out the balance between the two extremes and understanding how the Planner works, but it is in understanding that we have been given access to the Planner himself. The key to finding God's plan for our lives is found in *relationship*. God is our Father and His fatherhood is the key to realizing all He has planned and all He's given.

God has a plan for our children, but in order for them to walk into that plan fully, they need to be in relationship with God. When God gave them life—creating them individually and uniquely—and developed a plan for them—giving them talents, abilities, and personality types to equip them for that plan—He went one step further: He didn't leave them alone in that plan; He gave them Himself as their Father. He guides and directs them; He will help them get there. He will teach, train, correct, protect, love, and guide them and be their Father. What an awesome thing!

And God knows how your children function. He knows them completely, understands how His plan and design for them fit together. And the great news that all of this incorporates their desires and free will.

Trust

An essential part of every relationship is trust. God loves us completely and can be trusted every step of the way. *"Trust in the Lord with all your heart and lean not on your own understanding; in all your ways acknowledge him, and he will make your paths straight"* (Proverbs 3:5–6). *"Delight yourself in the Lord and he will give you the desires of your heart. Commit your way to the Lord; trust in him and he will do this"* (Psalm 37:4–5).

Six times in the Gospels Jesus said, *"Whoever wants to save his life will lose it, but whoever loses his life for me will find it"* (Matthew 16:25; see also Matthew 10:39; Mark 8:35; Luke 9:24, 17:33; John 12:25). When we lose our lives by giving them over to our Father in complete trust and choosing His way, rather than our own wants and desires, we gain our lives back. Remember that God is love, and everything He asks of us or wants us to do is best for us. He is committed to being our loving Father and caring for us—and for our children (they are His children too, because He has no grandchildren or stepchildren).

When our children give their lives to God, they put themselves in the best possible care—the care of One whose only motivation is their good and Who is fully capable of bringing that good to pass. Therefore, by losing their lives or trusting them to God, they truly gain them. In contrast, when they try to take care of themselves, make their own decisions, and follow their own plans, they lose their lives; because, they don't know the first thing about how they were made, what their talents are, what the future holds, or even what would truly make them happy.

If we try to help our kids find their way through life by means of any of the seven career motivators mentioned above, we give them limited (though well meant) advice at best. God's plan incorporates the full range of their talents, gifts, personalities, and so on; He takes *everything* into account.

I (Rick) said to God the day I became a Christian, "My life is Yours. I will do whatever You want." It was the best possible prayer I could ever have prayed. If I had written down all my gifts, desires, talents, and everything about me, and put it into a computer program that would spit out what I would do for the rest of my life, it couldn't even have come close to what I'm doing today. Every part of me, everything that excites me, every one of my gifts, everything about me—my past, present, and future—all seem to be considered in what I'm doing today. I give my life to God every day, and He gives it back to me in incredible ways. God's calling for my life perfectly matches who I am.

When I (Larry) asked Christ into my life, I made a commitment to God that I would never again be deliberately disobedient. I promised the Lord, "Whatever You say, I will do to the best of my ability, even if it costs me everything." I firmly believe that not only must we accept Him as Savior but also as Lord; and, as Lord over our lives, He has the right to use us however He chooses. I made that commitment over twenty-five years ago, and I am constantly surprised how the Lord chooses to use me.

Teach your children to pray this: "God, I know Your way is best for me. You have a special calling for me. I want to follow You and get to know You." Teach them to go into that trusting relationship—because it is key.

Notes

1. Hewitt Associates LLC, Database of Employee Opinions (1993–1996).

2. A *CNN/USA Today*/Gallup Poll conducted August 22–25, 1997.

3. "Stress, Relaxation and Pleasure Amongst Office Workers," ARISE/Harris Survey, 1994.

4. *Youthview,* February 1996.

5. Sax, L.J.; Astin, A.W.; Korn, W.S.; Mahoney, K.M. *The American Freshman: National Norms for Fall 1996.* Los Angeles: Higher Education Research Institute, UCLA 1996.

6. *Youthview,* February 1997.

7. *Youthview,* December 1996.

8. *Youthview,* January 1997.

1. God plans to use our character and gifts in His specific plan for us; yet, we often imitate and compare ourselves to the standards of others. Who do your children compare themselves to? Whose standard might you be pushing them to conform to?

2. In our culture today, the dominant career motivator is money—with a trace of the past's achievement ethic and the do-what-you-love philosophy thrown in. Discuss the errors in these three ideas, as compared to God's plan.

3. Even the church can mislead us with the so-called spiritual approach to our calling. Review with your child that being a full-time Christian worker is a great calling, but it's no more important than any other.

4. Does your child lean toward the wrong motivations in regard to his or her calling? Talk about career, money, prestige, fame, and security in terms he or she can understand, and compare those things to God's plan and design for him or her.

5. Oftentimes the path ahead looks difficult, and though we can't figure out how God does His job, He engineers it all. Discuss the specific ways that God works within His sovereignty to bring your child success.

6. What kind of relationship does your child have with God? Does he or she understand His Fatherly role in our lives: teaching, training, correcting, protecting, loving, and guiding us? Explain in-depth these aspects of our relationship with God.

7. It is difficult to fully comprehend how we can save our lives by losing them. Explain to your child how this concept relates to our sense of security and our decisions and plans, as we do things God's way.

Chapter 6

TALENTS, GIFTS, AND SPIRITUAL GIFTS

L ittle Joshua can sing with perfect pitch and play a song he's heard perfectly only once. Judy can add, multiply, and divide numbers in her head, while barely concentrating. Tina can draw lifelike and recognizable people with a few deft lines. Thomas can take anything mechanical apart and put it back together better than ever. Bobby can write a computer program that will do what he wants.

We say that these kids are talented or gifted, because they have abilities that set them apart from the rest of the average kids. The dictionary uses *talents, gifts,* and *abilities* interchangeably. But for the purpose of this book and to help us understand God's system for giving these abilities, we are going to define *talents* and *gifts* separately.

The natural abilities we have, as an integral part of who we are at birth, we will call our **talents.** Our talents can and should be trained and developed so we can use them to our fullest potential.

Throughout our lives, as we grow with God, He adds other abilities to us to help us as we seek to accomplish what He has given us to do. As we are faithful to grow in the talents He's given us, He gives us even more. These abilities, added throughout our lives, we are calling **gifts.** These gifts are similar to talents, but they are not given at birth. And there is no real limit to the number of gifts we can have. Like our natural talents, these gifts can be trained and developed.

Then there are the **spiritual gifts,** or manifestations, that God gives from time to time for particular purposes—to be used as needed. These are supernatural, instant helps for immediate use. Next time we are in similar situations, we may not have those spiritual gifts.

For example, if you need a word of wisdom, the ability to have a solution for a particular problem on the spot, it might come when you need help with a problem. But, the next time you face a problem you might not have the wisdom to know what to do, because spiritual gifts are not ours to keep. They are given as the Spirit wills for particular purposes and at specific moments in time.

Now let's look at these three in greater detail.

Natural Talents

Natural talents seem to be genetic to some degree. We often see that things like musical, intellectual, or mathematical abilities run in families. A mother and her son are musical; a father and his daughter excel at math. It seems that, as God knits each person together in the womb, He gives a person with the genetic talent for music a spirit that matches that talent. He also matches it to the person's individual personality, personality type, and so on, so that each person is a unified whole.

There seems to be a huge reservoir of possible talents that we could have. God picks some out of this reservoir to put into our individual talent "containers" in order to bless us, our families, our communities, and even the world. And He usually gives us more than one talent; we get them in sets, like good china. And the pattern of our set of talents is as unique as we are.

To some degree, the Bible corroborates that talents are genetic. *"Adah gave birth to Jabal; he was the father of those who live in tents and raise livestock. His brother's name was Jubal; he was the father of all who play the harp and flute. Zillah also had a son, Tubal-Cain, who forged all kinds of tools out of bronze and iron"* (Genesis 4:20–22).

This seems to indicate that these talents were passed down through the family line. They were part of the physical makeup God had designed for them—for their benefit and the benefit of the world.

We also see natural talents in Exodus as the Israelites made the Tabernacle. *"Every skilled woman spun with her hands and brought what she had spun. . . . And all the women who were willing and had the skill spun the goat hair"* (Exodus 35:25–26).

We also read, *"See, the Lord has chosen Bezalel son of Uri, the son of Hur, of the tribe of Judah, and he has filled him with the Spirit of God, with skill, ability and knowledge in all kinds of crafts—to make artistic designs for work in gold, silver and bronze, to cut and set stones, to work in wood and to engage in all kinds of artistic craftsmanship. And he has given both him and Oholiab son of Ahisamach, of the tribe of Dan, the ability to teach others. He has filled them with skill to do all kinds of work as craftsmen, designers, embroiderers in blue, purple and scarlet yarn and fine linen, and weavers—all of them master craftsmen and designers. So Bezalel, Oholiab and every skilled person to whom the Lord has given skill and ability to know how to carry out all the work of constructing the sanctuary are to do the work just as the Lord has commanded"* (Exodus 35:30–36:1).

Some people are given an extraordinary amount of talent, to the point of *genius,* which the dictionary defines as "a single strongly marked capacity or aptitude." In order to affect the lives of thousands of people, to improve life on this earth, or to accomplish some special task, sometimes God gives an extraordinary amount of a particular talent, or genius, in whatever area it is needed.

For example, a present-day mathematical genius is Stephen Hawking, who is following in the footsteps of Einstein. Some people have kinesthetic genius that has to do with physical ability and activity. We might say that Wayne Gretzky is a physical genius in his amazing understanding of hockey, as is Michael Jordan in basketball. Edison was a mechanical genius, as were the Wright brothers. Someone like Robin Williams or Billy Crystal have comedic genius. The list is almost endless.

As we look back through history or even as we look around at our world, we can see the evidence of talents and genius at work. Take the simple, everyday commodity of bread. At some point in history someone with the talent for it had to come up with the whole process of how we progress from grain growing in a field to the loaf of bread on the table. Who figured out that you could take this strange bacteria called yeast, add it to flour, knead and knead it, then leave it to rise, knead it again, and bake it? It's a complicated process that couldn't have happened accidentally. Someone, at some point in time, had the talent for experimentation or understanding the working of yeast and flour and then put the two together into the staple that is probably familiar to almost every living person.

Or look at clothes. How did people figure out how to get from the raw material to the woven result that we all wear? Imagine looking at a sheep grazing in the field and thinking warm wooly socks. Or looking at a cotton plant and thinking dresses, shirts, and pants. Someone did. Who came up with knitting? Or, closer to where we are now, who had the talent to come up with the microchip, which is almost as much a part of every household these days as that loaf of bread or the clothing?

We need to be careful not to limit our view of talents. Sometimes, when we see our child can't sing, act, or play sports well, we think he or she is not talented. That's not necessarily true. Einstein's parents probably almost despaired of him as he flunked out of math classes and repeatedly got lost on his way home. Amy Grant was told at one point that her talent definitely was not in the area of music. Many a best-selling author was told at some point that he or she couldn't write. So, we need to encourage our children to continue exploring their talents.

We also must be careful when we emphasize the more spectacular forms of talent. Few of us have genius-level talents, and not many of our kids do. God seems to have called a lot of "average" people with "average" talents. But the most important talents from God's perspective may not be the ones our society thinks are important. From a Christian perspective, the talents that matter most are the ones that may be the least visible or valued by the world around us.

Take a look at some of the talents listed in Romans 12 and 1 Corinthians 12: serving, teaching, encouraging, generosity or contributing to others' needs, leadership, showing mercy, helping others, administration. Our society can understand teaching, leadership, administration, and even generosity, but serving? showing mercy? helping others? Those are nice talents, people around us might say, but you don't make a lot of money or impress a lot of people with them!

Yet they are talents that are essential to the building of God's kingdom and helping families, the church, and society function. They are as important as any of the other talents we usually think of: music, sports, math, science, and so on. Mother Teresa is a perfect example of someone who used her talents of serving, helping, and showing mercy to the least of God's children. She exemplified the verse: *"Do you see a man skilled in his work? He will serve before kings; he will not serve before obscure men"* (Proverbs 22:29).

The point is not to compare our kids with other kids who may have more or fewer talents in a particular area or even in several areas. The point is that God has given each of our children talents that fit His plans and purposes for them. Our task as parents is to help them develop what they have.

Training Talents

Encourage your children not to bury the talents God gives them, as the Parable of the Talents in Matthew 25:14–28 shows. They can train and develop their talents. It's possible to translate the famous verse in Proverbs, *"Train a child in the way he should go, and when he is old he will not turn from it"* (Proverbs 22:6), with a somewhat different emphasis: "Train a child according to his or her bent." So train them not only in godly character but in accordance to the way God made them and the talents He's given them.

There's the temptation to take for granted a talent that allows us to do something easily. If we don't have to put out a lot of effort to learn math, or Latin, or whatever we're naturally good at, we don't really apply ourselves and end up doing far less with our talent than we could and should. It's good to learn a variety of things, and it can be fun, but we need to use and develop those things we have a natural talent for and keep moving forward with them, to the point of excellence. We should learn to use our talents to the very best of our abilities. This involves training, taking lessons, practicing, and developing in our talents in any way we can.

Children should always be pushing for excellence in all areas of their lives, like Daniel and his friends. *"To these four young men God gave knowledge and understanding of all kinds of literature and learning. . . . In every matter of wisdom and understanding about which the king questioned them, he found them ten times better than all the magicians and enchanters in his whole kingdom*" (Daniel 1:17, 20).

These young men trusted God for wisdom and help and excelled in whatever they tried to do. So should our kids, but they should excel especially in the areas of their talents, because God has given them for a reason.

However, this does not mean that your children's talents will necessarily be the focus of their careers or the center of their lives. For example, because your children are talented musically, it doesn't mean that they will be the next Amy Grant, Marvin Hamlisch, or Mozart. But it could be something they could use throughout their lives: singing in the choir, accompanying children, singing at weddings, writing music, teaching others, or just singing for the family.

Talents are from God, so they should be developed, whether they become careers or not. A specific talent doesn't necessarily lead to one career as a matter of course. For one thing, there are a number of ways any talent can be used. A talent for written communication, for example, does not automatically mean a career as a novelist or a newspaper columnist. It could take the form of writing plays, political speeches, sermons, brochures, sales materials, or just wonderful, encouraging letters to friends.

Only our relationship with God, not our talents, can truly give the direction our lives should go. But as God created us as a whole and gave us our talents purposely, they could be the way to point us toward our goals. It's the same way that choosing godly character helps us go down the right road to find God's plan and make the right choices. Developing our talents will direct our steps and then, when we need those talents, we'll have them fine-tuned and ready.

Gifts

Some time ago it was popular for people to wear buttons proclaiming "PBPWMGINFWMY." This stood for, "Please Be Patient with Me, God Is Not Finished with Me Yet." We are all on a journey to greater Christlikeness. Just as God is helping us develop godly character, and just as we need to develop our talents, we also need to keep developing our abilities throughout our lives. God doesn't give us everything at our birth; He also gives us gifts along the way. When we are in situations in which God wants us to do something that doesn't fit what we can do naturally, He gives us gifts to help us through. These gifts are then ours to continue to develop, fine-tune, and put to use.

Gifts are similar to talents, except that they are not part of us at birth. They are added to the blueprint of who we are later. But they are not added as in, "Oops, I guess I need to find somewhere to stick this." Rather, they were part of the blueprint all along, like a model that is built in stages. God knows from the beginning that between when we're born and when we die there will be a lot of space filled with living. In that space, relationship with God happens, and in the context of that relationship we need, and are given, gifts and abilities to help us accomplish the things He has designed for us to do.

God helps us train and increase our natural talents, as well as the new gifts He gives us. He wants us to be growing forever, even throughout eternity. And it would not be surprising that what we see as genius today will be more like wobbly toddler steps in eternity, when we are all continuing to explore and grow in our talents and gifts and as we continue to be given more gifts to use and enjoy. Isn't that something to look forward to?

Imagine parents who go away for a week, leaving their two-year-old child behind. They set out all the meals for the week and all the changes of clothing that the child will need while they're gone, arranged neatly by day. Of course, no parent would do that! We're well aware that a two-year-old wouldn't know what to do with those things, no matter how neatly they were arranged. Instead, parents need to give children things as they grow and as they need them.

You wouldn't give your seven-year-old the training and ability to drive a car. He or she's not ready for that yet. In a similar way, God gives us some things at the beginning of our lives, but He also knows that there are a lot of things He'll have to provide the ability for later—things we're not ready for yet. *"Everyone who has will be given more, and he will have an abundance. Whoever does not have, even what he has will be taken from him"* (Matthew 25:29). *"You have been faithful with a few things; I will put you in charge of many things"* (Matthew 25:21).

When we take the talents God has given us and push toward excellence, He honors us by giving us even more.

When I (Larry) began to teach on money management, I was given the gift of being able to talk in front of people and teach in a way that really worked. I think I had the talent to teach, but to actually get up in front of people to teach was a gift from God. I would walk out on stage, depending on God to help me to know what to say to that particular group. It thrilled me that I knew I was saying exactly what the group needed to hear. The more I did this, the more I grew in this gift.

It also used to startle me, since I wasn't a very good counselor, that I was able to give people more than just money answers to their problems. There was no way I could have done this without God's help. I began to depend on this gift that God was giving me and saw it as God's confirmation that I was doing the right thing.

The Bible gives us examples of these additional gifts. As mentioned previously, there's the Parable of the Talents in Matthew 25:14–28, in which the talent the lazy servant buried was given to the one who had received five talents.

Also, Paul told Timothy, *"Do not neglect your gift, which was given you through a prophetic message when the body of elders laid their hands on you"* (1 Timothy 4:14). Obviously, whatever this gift was—probably a special gift to be able to teach and to pastor—it was not given to Timothy at birth. It was added to him as he grew with God.

When God spoke to Moses from the burning bush and told him to go talk to Pharaoh, he said, *"O Lord, I have never been eloquent, neither in the past nor since you have spoken to your servant. I am slow of speech and tongue"* (Exodus 4:10).

Yet, later, Stephen said, *"Moses was educated. . .and was powerful in speech and action"* (Acts 7:22). So it wasn't that Moses couldn't speak. It seems that, if we look into what the Hebrew words mean and study the commentaries, Moses meant that he was not eloquent in his ability to go back and forth between Hebrew and Egyptian and convince Pharaoh and the Israelites. He didn't have "the gift of gab."

Moses was pointing to the fact that this was not a natural talent of his. God's response is revealing. *"Who gave man his mouth? Who makes him deaf or mute? Who gives him sight or makes him blind? Is it not I, the*

Lord? Now go; I will help you speak and will teach you what to say" (Exodus 4:11–12).

God is saying that He made us, with our talents and abilities and all the things we can or cannot do. God told Moses that He would help him. That seems to indicate that there's another kind of talent—the gift that God gives along the way as we go through life. God *added* the gift Moses really needed to accomplish the task God had given him.

On occasion, there are special gifts—like Daniel's. *"Daniel could understand visions and dreams of all kinds"* (Daniel 1:17). This gift of understanding dreams and visions was given to Daniel. But it seems that God's Spirit came along and added to that gift a special extra ability at the right time-the special gift of the ability to interpret the king's dream. Although Daniel was given a gift to understand dreams, he said, *"No wise man, enchanter, magician or diviner can explain to the king the mystery he has asked about, but there is a God in heaven who reveals mysteries"* (Daniel 2:27). In other words, only God could have given him the interpretation.

Bezalel and Oholiab, in Exodus 35, were talented craftsmen, but we read that God also gave them extra abilities to understand and organize the whole project and to teach the other artisans. *"[The Lord] has filled them with skill to do all kinds of work. . . . So Bezalel, Oholiab and every skilled person to whom the Lord has given skill and ability. . .are to do the work just as the Lord has commanded"* (Exodus 35:35–36:1).

God has an incredible "gift bag" full of wonderful things for us: talents, extra gifts, and special gifts to accomplish God's purposes. As we get to know God, we gain understanding of these wonderful things God has available for us. He can only give them to us as we're ready, as we grow in character, remain faithful in the other things He's given us, and continue to develop and use the talents and gifts He gives us.

Encourage your child not to fall into the "Moses trap" of saying, "I can't do this because I don't have the talent for it." God will take your children through all kinds of stages as they obey Him and walk with Him. And they can trust Him to provide whatever they need (they'll learn this as they go). In fact, as they develop these gifts, they might find somewhere down the road that the gifts become their strongest assets and the clearest directions on the road to God's destination for them.

The apostle Paul said, *"I can do everything through him who gives me strength"* (Philippians 4:13). He also said, *"For when I am weak, then I am strong"* (2 Corinthians 12:10).

Spiritual Gifts

There are spiritual gifts that God gives to accomplish specific tasks. These spiritual gifts don't stay with us; they aren't ours in the same way that talents and gifts are. The Holy Spirit gives these spiritual gifts to use for specific purposes—to help in particular situations—as needed. *"Now to each one the manifestation of the Spirit is given for the common good"* (1 Corinthians 12:7).

The Greek word for "spiritual gifts" in that verse is actually "manifestations," which indicates that these are really evidences of the Holy Spirit working in peoples' lives, rather than gifts that are given to keep and to use. Rather, these things belong to God's Spirit to use when and where He will, through people who are willing and available.

Churches have different ideas about how these gifts are manifested and how they function in the church today. Throughout the Bible, God has always shown Himself more powerful than we can even imagine, and He does things that go beyond our abilities and understanding. He's done this by working through and with individuals. The key is that *God is not limited by the things that limit us.* And He is able and will do anything He needs to do to get a job done.

Word of Knowledge. The Spirit gives us special knowledge of things we could not know by ourselves. For example, Jesus looked into a tree one day and said, *"Zacchaeus, come down immediately"* (Luke 19:5). Jesus knew his name even though He had never met him before. He also seemed to know that Zacchaeus was a lonely, ostracized man, because Jesus invited Himself to go to Zacchaeus' home.

God, who knows everything, can share some of His knowledge when it will be helpful and encouraging or when a person needs to be gently called to task on something. Jesus' recognition and friendliness caused Zacchaeus to turn his whole life around.

Word of Wisdom. Sometimes the Spirit gives us wisdom about what to do in a situation—wisdom we don't have. This gift often helps us apply the Bible to situations we or someone else is facing. Peter, when taken before the religious leaders, after healing the lame man at the Gate Beautiful, showed them how Psalm 118:22 spoke of Jesus. The leaders knew that Peter was just a simple fisherman with little formal education and they were amazed at his insight (see Acts 4:11–13). Often this gift can come when we are counseling someone or when we are in a situation in which wisdom is badly needed. Suddenly we have a new insight into what approach to take.

Many times when I (Larry) was counseling with people, and they were going over a problem that was too complicated for me to understand, I would stop and suggest we pray. They thought I was praying for them. I wasn't. I was praying for me. *"If any of you lacks wisdom, he should ask God, who gives generously to all without finding fault, and it will be given to him"* (James 1:5).

I would ask God for the wisdom I needed to help these people. When I would feel the answer inside and begin to explain it to them, it was as much a revelation to me as to them. It was the right answer and it was remarkable. There was no way I could have come up with it. It had to be from God—God speaking through me. He wasn't using my background or knowledge; He was simply using me as a vessel through whom He could speak.

Discernment of Spirits. This gift tells us whether something is from God, from a person's own mind and heart, or from evil spirits. Jesus knew that the man who said, *"You are . . . the Holy One of God!"* (see Mark 1:23–28) was not saying it because God had told him that. Instead, he was saying it under the inspiration of an evil spirit.

Peter knew that when Simon the sorcerer asked, *"Give me also this ability so that everyone on whom I lay my hands may receive the Holy Spirit,"* his motives were wrong (see Acts 8:19). He wanted it for money and because of the bitterness in his heart. When Peter confronted Simon, telling him that his heart was not right before God, Simon repented. *"Pray to the Lord for me so that nothing you have said may happen to me"* (Acts 8:24).

Gifts of healing. These are gifts given to us on behalf of sick people. People brought their sick into the streets so that Peter's shadow would fall on them. And when it did they were healed (see Acts 5:12–16). *"Is any one of you sick? He should call the elders of the church to pray*

over him and anoint him with oil in the name of the Lord. And the prayer of-
fered in faith will make the sick person well; the Lord will raise him up"
(James 5:14–15).

Miracles. Miracles are things that are impossible for us to do on our
own. Often they seem to go against the established understanding of
how the world works. This is why science has a great deal of difficulty
believing in miracles, even the ones recorded in Scripture. Jesus turned
water into wine at a wedding in Cana, His first miracle after beginning
His ministry (see John 2:1–11).

The apostle Paul caused an evil man, Elymas the sorcerer, to go
blind when he tried to turn the proconsul of Cyprus away from God
and keep him from becoming a Christian (see Acts 13:4–12). Often
miracles are used to confirm to people that God is real or to show that a
person is truly speaking on God's behalf.

Faith. God gives us the ability to trust Him when times are tough.
He gives us an extra dose of faith that helps us through a tough time,
helps us obey, or helps us persevere. Noah believed God when He said
there would be a flood, even though it had never even rained like that
before. He worked for close to one hundred years to build the ark
because of his faith. Faith which was, of course, amply rewarded (see
Genesis 6–9).

Hebrews 11 gives us numerous examples of people of faith. Abraham had faith in God when God promised to give Abraham and his descendants the land where Abraham was only a visitor. He also believed
God when He told him that he (Abraham) would have descendants,
even though he and his wife were barren. *"Abram believed the Lord, and
he credited it to him as righteousness"* (Genesis 15:6).

Prophecy. In the New Testament, this is a message God gives or inspires us with to encourage people, make them stronger, and give them
hope and comfort (see 1 Corinthians 14:3). The writer of Proverbs
says, *"A word aptly spoken is like apples of gold in settings of silver"*
(Proverbs 25:11). The gift of prophecy inspires us with the right words,
at the right time, to speak to another's need.

Tongues. The New Testament does not seem to express clearly the
exact nature of the manifestation of tongues and of the interpretation of
tongues, and there has been much debate over their use and relevance.

Some feel that there is a tongue prayer language that is distinct from the gift of tongues. But one thing is certain. If God can speak through a donkey and use a huge fish to redirect a prophet, He can cause us to speak in other known or unknown languages if needed.

The Spirit gives some people the ability to speak in a language they haven't learned and don't understand (for an example, see Acts 2:4).

Interpretation of Tongues. If the gift of tongues is used in public meetings, it needs to be interpreted so that everyone can benefit from it. Read about Paul's teaching on this gift in 1 Corinthians 14:27-28.

All of these gifts are given to make the body of Christ stronger and to help us spread God's kingdom through the world. God loves people and wants to draw them to Himself. These gifts are usually given to help in that task. Through these gifts God leads us closer to Him and to each other, as we encourage and help one another.

We cannot really train our children in these gifts, but we can make sure they understand what they are and their purposes. And we can encourage them to be willing and available to God.

You can explain it like this to your children: God knows everything, He is everywhere, and He can do anything. He's with us all the time, wanting to help us do whatever He has given us to do. Sometimes that may involve more of God and a lot less of ourselves. Our job is to be open to God and eager to help Him accomplish His purposes.

Teach them that God equips us with all that we'll need to fulfill His plans for our lives. He gives talents and gifts that are suited to who we are, how God designed us, and His direction for us. Then, as with everything else God has given us, we are responsible for using and developing these talents and gifts.

God has designed it all, given it all, as a unified whole that perfectly matches who He made us to be physically—the particular, individual spirit He has given that makes us who we are, the wonderful unique personality He has graced us with, and the personality type He's given so we fit well into the place He's planned for us in our communities.

Then He adds special talents and abilities, the tools we bring to our communities, the things that equip and suit us to our roles and that, when we learn to use them well, are of great benefit to our communities and others. All of these are pointing us to the path God has planned for us to walk down as we move into all He has for us to do and contribute.

Our job as parents is to help our children recognize and develop the talents God has given them and to teach them the attitude of growth that says we are continually learning and continually being equipped by God as we grow. In this way they will be able to say yes to any task God puts before them, saying with the apostle Paul, *"I can do everything through him who gives me strength"* (Philippians 4:13).

1. Describe the differences between natural talents, gifts, and spiritual gifts. How might they interweave in a given circumstance? Why do they not belong to us?

2. In what areas of their lives have your children not performed well at all? Have these failures affected your attitude toward their abilities in general? Or have you prematurely given up on your children?

3. Name some talents that are emphasized in God's plan for us but are not highly valued in our culture. How can we develop these as a priority over those that the world prizes?

4. Look at a basic talent like drawing or some other talent your child possesses. How could this talent be used for multiple (or different) purposes, other than the obvious one that comes to mind?

5. If spiritual gifts are not naturally present at birth like talents are, pick the gifts in your child that you think God is adding. How can you assist in the training process to be sure your child's gifts are truly developed?

6. Though you cannot train your child in spiritual gifts, review the list with him or her, while carefully explaining them and answering questions. Ask your child which gifts have the most appeal to him or her, and attempt to develop them within your child's home, church, and spiritual life.

7. Does your child realize that people who put little effort into the development and expression of their extraordinary gifts are not as laudable as someone who has lesser gifts, but gives his or her best effort to their development and expression? Talk about why this is so.

Chapter 7

FINDING
AND FOLLOWING
GOD'S WILL

We've established that God has a plan for us that takes into account all of who we are and that He cares about where we're going, because He has called us. But that's the big picture. What about this morning's decisions and this afternoon's decisions? Does God care about the little day-to-day things? Or does God just get involved in the big decisions: who to marry, what career choices to make, whether to have children, and when to change jobs? Before we can talk about actually finding and following God's will, we must first answer the following question.

Does God Care About the Small Things in Life?

The simple answer is that if we don't do each day what God wants us to do, we'll get to the end of our lives not knowing if we've done what He wanted.

Imagine a man determined to win a gold medal at the next Olympic games. That goal is posted on his bedroom wall, and stickers on the fridge remind him of his purpose. He buys the latest running shoes and streamlined shorts, guaranteed to cut down wind resistance. He even shaves his legs so that the wind resistance of the hairs won't slow him down. He tells all his friends of his ambition.

A couple of times a week, when he feels like it, he wanders down to the track to practice his running. He does some warm-up exercises to stretch his leg muscles; then he runs a couple of laps. He rests, has a cheeseburger and a milkshake, then runs a couple more laps. He spends the rest of his time napping, watching TV, snacking, and reading in the latest magazines about running.

When the Olympics come around, will he be on the team? Not likely. He had a great goal, but the everyday decisions he made and his day-to-day actions took him away from his goal.

It's the same with our lives. The small steps we take today determine where we'll end up. We can't take a few steps south every day and expect to find ourselves further north by the end of the week. So it stands to reason that if God is interested in where we'll end up, He is also interested in where we are heading today.

Let's take a look at several reasons why we know that God is interested in leading and guiding us daily.

1. God Is Not a Part-Time Dad. God wants to be our Father on a daily basis; He doesn't want to be a part-time dad. The Bible is clear about this. *"If anyone loves me, he will obey my teaching. My Father will love him, and we will come to him and make our home with him"* (John 14:23). *"God has said, 'Never will I leave you; never will I forsake you'"* (Hebrews 13:5). Jesus and His Father, our Father, are constantly with us.

You would never think of leaving an infant child alone with the admonition, "You have a brain. Use it to figure out how life works." Babies need to be trained in how to use their brains; they must be nurtured, loved, and cared for. They need to be taken through life one step at a time. Good parents spend time loving and nurturing their children.

God is the same; He doesn't run off and leave us to fend for ourselves. God is not an absentee parent. He is the ultimate parent. He initiated parenting.

When we are away from our children, it causes heartache. This inborn desire to be there for our kids comes from God's intense desire to be with us daily, loving and caring for us, helping, nurturing, teaching, and training us. Paul said, *"For this reason I kneel before the Father, from* whom his whole family in heaven and earth derives its name" (Ephesians 3:14–15).

God is also a gentle parent. Jesus regularly went away to spend long periods of time alone with His Father. We also need to expend some effort to respond to God. Jesus told His disciples when they fell asleep, *"Could you men not keep watch with me for one hour? . . . Watch and pray so that you will not fall into temptation. The spirit is willing, but the body is weak"* (Matthew 26:40–41). God will not automatically push His plans on us. Neither will He push His fathering or His wisdom on us. He wants us to come freely and trustingly, yielding ourselves to Him and His love.

2. God Wants Us to Pray Continuously. One way we come to God is in prayer. Throughout the Bible we see that God calls us to Him daily. *"It is good to praise the Lord . . . to proclaim your love in the morning and your faithfulness at night"* (Psalm 92:1–2). *"Do not be anxious about anything, but in everything, by prayer and petition, with thanksgiving, present your requests to God"* (Philippians 4:6). Paul said, *"Pray continually"* (1 Thessalonians 5:17).

It seems clear from this that God wants continual communion with us. That means He wants us to talk to Him about everything. He wants to direct us in everything, give us wisdom in everything, and help us grow in everything we face and experience. He wants ongoing, loving, intimate, and growing relationships with us. And through those relationships He will guide and direct us.

3. God Wants Us to Grow into Christlikeness. Most of us are aware of God's interest in our lives, at least when it comes to sin. We know God doesn't want us to sin. The trouble is that we often seem to think that God's only interest in us is to keep us from sinning. Thank the Lord, His interest is more positive than that. He also wants to show us what is right, not just in terms of sinning and not sinning but in terms of good and better choices.

The Holy Spirit wants to remind us of what Jesus taught us (see John 14:26). Christ Jesus has become wisdom from God—for us (see 1 Corinthians 1:30). The fact that Jesus is living with us shows us that God wants to give us His wisdom on an ongoing basis—so that we can grow and become like Him. This growth is the goal of our daily relationship with God.

"Therefore, my dear friends . . . continue to work out your salvation with fear and trembling, for it is God who works in you to will and to act according to his good purpose" (Philippians 2:12-13). God wants a daily involvement in our growth. And that means He will guide us in all our decisions, regardless of their size or significance.

4. The Holy Spirit Guides Us into Truth. If we're yielding ourselves to God He will guide us into truth. How does He do that? Well, we know that it doesn't happen overnight. It's not that one day we're non-Christians and the next we're saved and know all Christian truth. We need to be guided and led into it step-by-step, day-by-day. The reality is that we know a portion of Christian truth, and we try to apply that portion to our lives.

But there's a lot of other truth that we aren't applying to our lives. The Spirit of Truth dwells within us and leads and guides us further into that truth each day. The Bible tells us the Spirit will remind us of what Jesus taught, and He will tell us what is to come (see John 16:13). Jesus said, *"I have much more to say to you, more than you can now bear. But when he, the Spirit of truth, comes, He will guide you into all truth"* (John 16:12–13). Jesus knew we had to grow into truth. And He gave us the Holy Spirit to help us with that.

5. Biblical Examples. Look at figures in the Bible—from Adam and Eve to Noah, Moses, Samuel, Saul, David, Jonah, Jesus, Peter, and Paul. These people, about whom we teach Bible stories to our children, had active communication with God. They knew what God wanted them to do and where He wanted them to go. From Genesis to Revelation, God painted a picture for us of Him having active communion and leadership in the lives of His people.

"Jesus Christ is the same yesterday and today and forever" (Hebrews 13:8). God is the same as He always was. He doesn't change. He loves us and wants a daily, ongoing, intimate, involved relationship with us, just as He had with the people mentioned in the previous paragraph. God has promised to complete His work in us. *"The Lord will fulfill* [or perfect] *his purpose for me"* (Psalm 138:8). That means He has ongoing work to do. We can be sure He will do it if we allow Him to.

Learning Life One Step at a Time

If all of this is true, if God is so interested in directing us and being involved in our lives on a daily basis, why do some of us not get direction from God? Maybe it's because we don't believe that God wants to direct us today, so we don't trust Him for that. Or maybe we don't particularly *want* God to be involved in the details of our lives; we like the *idea* of trusting God a lot better than actually trusting Him. We say we are giving our lives to God, but unless we do this each day in everything—little and big—and with each decision—right or wrong, left or right—we're not really giving our lives to God at all.

I (Rick) was talking to a man who had a problem in his marriage. He told me he loved his wife so much that he'd jump in front of a truck to save her. He vowed he would give his life for her. I said, "Great! Then in the situation the two of you are fighting over right now, why don't you give some ground? Why don't you see her point, let her be right, and you change?" He reacted very strongly, saying, "Oh, no! I could never do that!"

He had just said he'd give his life for his wife, yet he wouldn't give an inch on this little point. I told him with assurance that when it came right down to it, if he had to sacrifice his life for his wife, he wouldn't. How did I know? Because he was not doing it in the little things. He wasn't giving to her with his pride, with his heart, or with the everyday things. And it is those little things that set the pattern of life, a pattern that would not change in the blink of an eye—or the rush of a truck.

It's the same with us and God. The pattern of our lives is set down in the little things. If we're not giving our lives to God each day with each decision, we are not giving our entire lives to Him. We are only allowing God to be involved in the big decisions.

You raise your children, pray for them, and teach them to make wise decisions based only on the pros and cons and the rational right and wrong of each choice. They grow up, making their own decisions. Then comes the day your daughter decides to marry Joey (or Max or Fred or . . .), or your son decides to become a dentist.

What would happen if you took your daughter aside and solemnly asked, "Have you prayed about this? Are you sure he is God's choice for you?" Or what would happen if you asked your son, "Have you prayed about being a dentist? Are you sure this is what God has for you?"

They'll look at you as if you're from another planet. If your daughter didn't pray about the dates she went on and who she dated and your son never prayed about the courses he took in high school, why would they do it now?

If your children haven't been taught to commit their lives and every decision to God, what makes you think they will suddenly commit these major decisions to God? She wants to marry Joey. He wants to enter dentistry. They have no experience of God leading them. The result? She'll marry Joey, and he'll become a dentist—no matter what God's plan was for her or him.

Patterns must be established in our children's lives. We need to teach them to go to God with every decision, beginning now. If they're trying to decide what to get Mom for Mother's Day, for example, we can suggest that they pray about it and ask for wisdom about what would make a nice present. This is not a matter of getting God's perfect direction for what gift to buy or having God tell them, "Buy this!" or "Do that for her!"

Asking for wisdom is simply asking God to help them think of a great gift. It's not a big deal. They don't have to pray passionately on their knees for hours. But simply teaching your children that God is interested in *everything* that concerns them, assuring them that He wants to give them wisdom, and setting them in the direction of constantly and automatically going to God, will establish a pattern for them to naturally go to God with the big decisions. They will develop a habit of looking to God for wisdom and for their personal growth. Then when major decisions arise, the answers will come.

Look at the analogy of pilots' training. Before pilots are allowed to fly airplanes, the airline puts them through an enormous amount of training. They spend a great deal of time in simulators, where they run repeatedly into every single problem that could occur in the air. It's true that 99.99 percent of those problems will never occur for any one pilot, but the airline wants to be sure that if pilots find themselves in those situations, the responses will be preconditioned and virtually automatic.

For example, if a pilot is flying in very bad, foggy weather and for some reason the plane suffers a microburst that flips it upside down, human instinct will tell him or her that up is down and down is up. Going by instinct, the pilot would do exactly the wrong thing. The airline teaches pilots to survive these microbursts by preconditioning them to look at their instruments and do only what the instruments tell them to do. They learn to ignore their senses.

By teaching our children to "fly by God's instruments" in their everyday lives, we can be sure that when they hit a microburst—some big decision or an unexpected and complicated problem—they will naturally go to God for His wisdom and "fly by His instruments." And they will come through with flying colors.

When children have this habit established in their lives, then when it comes to choosing a career or whom they should marry they will have been praying about it from the beginning. It will be understood that they have been praying about their decisions all along the way in their relationships and know what God's will is for them.

We need to ground our children in these words from a popular gospel song, "Day by day, three things I pray. To know thee more clearly, follow thee more nearly, and love thee more dearly." If this is our motto and we're preconditioning our kids to go to God in the little things, their hearts will become intertwined with God's. They'll stop and pray about decisions, wait for God's peace, and know what the right choices are.

If we haven't been doing this ourselves, or if we have older children who didn't receive this training, we can begin where they are, one decision at a time, to train them to go to God. The most effective way of teaching is modeling. We can tell our children we're going to be making decisions differently from now on. Then we can let them watch and be a part of our new decision-making process. When we encourage them to go to God, they'll have something practical to base it on and they'll understand what we mean.

The rest of this chapter will help you see how you can practically help and teach your children to commit to God's leading, give Him their lives, pray about things, and be sensitive to what God is saying and doing.

Seeds of Destiny

Okay, we've established now that God cares about the smallest details of our lives and of the lives of our children. We also know that it's important for our kids to learn to follow God's direction in the small things of life so that they will be able to fulfill their calling. But how can our children find and follow God's will?

When we talk about going to God for His leading, we're not saying that we should pray about everything; let God be the director of every decision; and then ignore all natural logic, wisdom, and preparation. God made this natural world and gave it to us. He invented planning, learning, and education. He gave us everything we have and matched it with purpose, and He gave us and our children talents and more gifts along the way to further prepare us for what we're to do.

These things are all significant. They all become *seeds of destiny* along the road that point out God's direction for us. For example, we can look at our personality types and see what suits certain kinds of jobs.

If your daughter is a high I (Influencer), she probably won't want to be a computer programmer who sits and works alone for days at a time. She'd be much better in some kind of people-oriented job. If God has given your son great gifts in the area of mathematics so that it comes easy to him, chances are that this ability will have something to do with where God wants him to be. This can be a seed of destiny, developing in a general direction.

When we look at all the natural factors and seeds of destiny and then look at submitting ourselves to God, we sometimes think these two—natural factors and God's will—are in conflict. But when we look at how God is sovereign from the time we are conceived, that He has lovingly designed every single part of us, and that He has equipped us for our lives, we realize that all the natural factors are important and not in conflict with God's will. They are not just seeds of destiny, they are *signposts from God.*

It can be helpful to take an inventory of these natural things, like what personality types we are, and what talents and gifts we have. These are things God has intentionally, purposely given us. We need to work on them, grow in them, and use them to help us find where we are to go. They are all part of the way God leads us.

Some decisions about how to train and what direction to go in are clear. If our children have great musical gifts, we don't need to ask God if they should develop these gifts. Of course they should; this is a very clear signpost. The question should be, rather, how do we help them develop their gifts? What direction should they take? singing? piano? a combination?

It's the same thing with kinesthetic ability. Some children are amazingly capable in sports and physical activities from a very young age. Rather than asking if this talent is somehow linked with what God has for them, we should be asking for wisdom in how to develop it.

These natural seeds of destiny work together with God's calling and care. Our personality types, likes and dislikes, talents and gifts all lead us in God's direction. When we put these together with our knowledge that God wants to be our Father, giving us help and direction day by day, we realize it's harder to lose our way than to find it.

God often plants seeds in our kids' hearts that are hints about what they will be and where they will go. These are extra seeds of destiny. Some studies show, and psychologists have found, that around the age of 12 there's something in a child's heart that steers him or her in a direction. It's something that causes them to say, "I would really like to . . . ."

I (Larry) remember that my goals were somehow set in my heart when I was very young. I can remember that I was not tall enough to reach up and turn the faucets on, but I had my long-term goals set. I was going to get an education, no matter what, because in my mind it was the key to success. That was preset in my mind at an early age, and it never changed. This seed of destiny helped to steer my direction later in life.

Another seed of destiny in my (Larry's) life is that I knew for a long time that there was one thing I was going to do better than anyone else in the world. Much later, I remember being at a roundtable discussion with a lot of very well-known and respected biblical scholars. They were asking me questions about biblical principles of finance and money management. I realized at that moment that this was one thing I did better than anyone else. I realized that, "In the land of the blind the one-eyed man is king." I was in the land of the blind and I could see.

At that time no one was teaching and studying the Bible's financial principles, so I was the best at it. That has changed now. There are many others working in this field and even doing a better job. But God had fulfilled that seed of destiny in me. That was definitely a confirmation that I was doing what God wanted me to do.

I (Rick) was watching a television show when I was 10 or 11 years old. One of the characters had a job working for an advertising agency. He had to come up with ad campaign ideas for pitching a product. In this episode, he struggled with it, then came up with an idea everyone liked. I thought, *Wow! To be able to think up ideas would be the coolest job!* I was so impacted by this that I started purposely applying my mind to coming up with ideas to solve problems. I remember lying awake in bed at night, inventing things.

That was a seed of destiny. God planted something there, and if you look at what I do now, running Lightwave, which creates new products and programs that will help parents pass on their faith to their children, a big part of my job is coming up with the ideas. I recalled that seed God planted years ago when, recently, a colleague called me "the Johnny Appleseed of ideas."

We can be watching for these seeds of destiny in our children's lives. We should encourage them in these areas, but we should be careful about taking these seeds of destiny too imminently. If I (Rick) had tried to turn this into something specific too soon, I probably would have gone into advertising.

It's important for us to have open dialogues with our children about their desires and what they would like to do or be when they grow up. Yes, we can affirm that God has a plan for their lives, but by allowing them to discuss their feelings and thoughts we show them that God, who created them, matched them perfectly to what He has called them to do and be.

Their desires are important and can be significant seeds of destiny. And we don't have to worry; their desires will change and grow with them. (It's always easier to understand the meaning of God's seeds of destiny in hindsight.)

Finding God's Will

Let's assume that our children are going to God daily with big things and little things. They have their signposts and their seeds of destiny. But how do they practically go forward to find God's will? And how do we help them find it? Our foundational Scripture for this is, *"Trust in the Lord with all your heart and lean not on your own understanding; in all your ways acknowledge him, and he will make your paths straight"* (Proverbs 3:5–6). These verses show us three simple, but strong, foundations we can teach our kids: *trust, commit,* and *follow.*

1. Trust

"Trust in the Lord with all your heart." Since you can't trust someone whose character you don't know, we have to help our children trust God and establish a trusting, growing relationship with Him. We need to give our children the deeply embedded confidence that God's character is loving and reliable.

It's important to teach your children that God has a special plan and a special purpose for their lives. They need the confidence that God loves them uniquely and is in control. And they must know that God will lead them and guide them as they get to know Him. In short, they need to know that they can trust God implicitly, completely, and without reservation.[1]

Even when your children are very young you can tell them, "God loves you. He has a special plan for you. He has something wonderful for you to do." These are basic foundation stones that must be laid level and solid in their lives, because it's on these things that their lives will be built. It is the unwavering assurance of God's character and God's regard that helps to set the pattern that will determine who they will be and how they will live.

The second part of our foundational verse says, *"And lean not on your own understanding"* (Proverbs 3:5). Assure your children that God is bigger than they are. He sees the whole picture, like a topographical map of their lives, when they can't see over the next hill.

Explain that they can continue to trust God even when it doesn't look like things are going the right way. When that happens, they can stop and tell God they've put themselves into His hands and know that

He is faithful. They can tell Him they know that He's in charge, that He loves them, and that His plan is the best. *"We know that in all things God works for the good of those who love him, who have been called according to his purpose"* (Romans 8:28).

Part of leaning on our own understanding is trying to determine the next step for ourselves. There's nothing wrong with planning and looking at the seeds of destiny God has given, but we must keep our eyes on God and lean on His understanding, rather than on our own.

There will be times when things happen that we or our children don't understand. It might not look like God is involved, but we know that we can always trust that He has control of our lives. Also, He is bigger than our mistakes. We can be redeemed if we ask for forgiveness and trust Him to put us back on track. God has a way of working it all into good so that, looking back later, it looks as if even our mistakes, or the difficult circumstances, were all part of God's plan. God can use different ways to bring all of us to where He wants, but He loves to turn the enemy's ploys, or our own mistakes, into blessings.

It comes down to this: No matter what happens, when it looks like God has forgotten us or our children, when it seems that our lives are off track, or when trouble or sickness or any other disappointments come, God *is* in control. God can and will turn *anything* around and use it to accomplish His purposes in our lives. God is a creative weaver of life; He can take any thread—even one that seems to be added randomly and out of sync, one that doesn't seem to fit the pattern at all or that is completely the wrong color—and He can weave it into an intricate, beautiful addition to His overall pattern. We can trust Him for that. Help your children understand these things.

2. Commit

"In all your ways acknowledge him" (Proverbs 3:6). Teach your children that one way to acknowledge God daily, decision by decision, and to commit their ways to Him is through prayer. Assure them that God is listening to them, because He wants to care for them and everything they turn over to Him. They can talk to Him about everything; they can give it all over to Him and trust Him with it. There is nothing too big or too little for God to care about. If your children need wisdom, teach

them to ask God. When they have problems with friends, or anything else, encourage them to take it to God.

As parents, we can be our children's "answers-to-prayer watchers." First, we help them commit all the different aspects of their lives to God: the little things, the bigger things, the places where they need wisdom or direction, the things they need God to help them work out, the lessons they want help with, or the tests they're taking, and so on. Then we watch for the answers.

When you see God working things out, draw your children's attention to the answers. God doesn't always answer immediately, so often your children don't make the connection between their prayers and God's answers. Help them to recognize God at work in their lives. This reinforces God's love and the benefits of committing things to Him. Also, when you point out an answer to prayer, remind them to say "Thank You" to God in prayer that night.

When we are young, life is simple. As we get older, life gets more complicated and the decisions we have to make get progressively more involved; there are more factors involved and our responsibilities increase. So when we teach our children at an early age how to commit the simplest problems to God and ask God for wisdom in the simplest things, it's a natural progression that, as they grow and their lives get more complicated with more responsibilities, they will apply those same principles to the next level. And to every level after that.

By the time they are adults leading complex lives with a whole array of things to deal with, they will have a solid resource base of trusting God, leaning on Him, and looking to Him for wisdom and direction. They will have a history of knowing God cares for what they commit to Him. Turning things over to God will be their automatic response. *"Train a child in the way he should go, and when he is old he will not turn from it"* (Proverbs 22:6). God's way will be their default.

3. Follow

"He will make your paths straight" (Proverbs 3:6). Once your children have trusted God and committed things to Him, God will "make their paths straight." He will direct them and they can follow in the path He

has prepared for them. How do they do this? There are five things you can teach your children that will help them find and follow God's will.

a. God's Written Word. God created everything in life to work according to His character. The principles that tell us how this life works are laid down in His Word. God designed us to match His character and fit into life according to these same principles. So, when He looked forward and designed His plan for our children, He naturally did it all according to His character and His principles and, therefore, according to righteousness. That means that He planned and foresaw a path for them that had to do with them making right choices and abiding by His principles and His Word.

The foundational way God leads is through righteousness, through what God has already said is the right way to do things and the right way to live, as laid out in the Bible. He has told us clearly in His Word what He wants from us. It is important that you teach your children the need to be faithful in the basics before God will give them more specific direction for their lives. When they make decisions according to God's Word and character, they are choosing to be like God and they're choosing to stay on His path—not just the "path of the righteous" but their particular, personal path, because God's path for them is consistent with the path of righteousness.

The easiest and most basic way that you can help your children follow God's path for their lives is to teach them to do things God's way. Whenever a decision involves right and wrong, choosing right will automatically keep them on God's path. Choosing wrong will take them off of it. This is why it is so important to teach your kids to read the Bible and to read it regularly. They must know and understand what's the right way—God's way—to live and do things.[2]

"He who is faithful with little is put over much" (see Matthew 25:14–30). When we follow God's principles in the little things, we're given more. But when we don't, we end up with even less. To explain this to your children, you might use the example of when they're tempted to tell "little white lies." Faced with the temptation, they might conclude that if they tell lies they'll get off scot-free, but if they tell the truth they'll get in trouble.

This seems like a simple issue, but if they make the wrong decisions and tell the "little white lies" that seem so innocent, they knock themselves off course. As a result they are no longer in accordance with how God created them, how He created the world, and how He set their pathways and the plan for their lives to go. Every time they make detours off God's path for them, if they keep on making wrong decisions, they'll get further and further away from God's plans for them. Soon they'll find that they are nowhere near the paths God wants them on.

"The righteousness of the blameless makes a straight way for them, but the wicked are brought down by their own wickedness. The righteousness of the upright delivers them, but the unfaithful are trapped by evil desires" (Proverbs 11:5–6). *"In the way of righteousness there is life; along that path is immortality"* (Proverbs 12:28). *"Righteousness guards the man of integrity, but wickedness overthrows the sinner"* (Proverbs 13:6).

The same general principle that the airlines use to train their pilots can help you raise your children. A lot of the situations they are going to face in the future will leave them confused or afraid, if they aren't prepared. Like the airlines, you should make your children aware of those situations and go over them time after time, teaching them what the Bible says, so that they'll know how to respond. Then, whatever the situations might be (for example temptations to lie or steal), they will have been exposed to it and to God's Word repeatedly, so they'll be preconditioned with the right response. They'll respond according to what God's Word says, not according to what their natural human instinct would dictate. This, incidentally, is also why it is important to have your kids memorize Bible verses. It's a form of preparation for what is to come.

Let's look at the example of finances. Let's say we precondition our children that borrowing is abnormal and that, whatever decisions they're making, they should walk away and pray about them for a period of time—maybe 24 hours—before deciding. Then, when they're older and this "super good deal" comes up—whether it's buying a car or investing in some get-rich-quick plan—rather than responding according to the human perspective of having to make quick decisions, they won't. They'll take the time to pray about it. This is preconditioning. We put our children through the simulator, even though they may not have faced the situations yet.

Sometimes we think that we'll get ahead by cheating on our income tax or by compromising God's standards in some other area or decision. But when we do this we are not weaseling our way ahead; we're weaseling our way right out of God's wonderful plan for our lives. We've taken control of our own lives, thinking we know better than God. In reality we are messing with our own future. We haven't followed the simplest path God has given us for our own good: His Word. God will never, *never* lead us to do something that goes contrary to His written Word, and you should be sure your children are secure in that fact.

b. The Conscience. A healthy conscience is hooked up to the right way of doing things. The more we get to know God, the more accurate our consciences become. The conscience shows us when we're about to do something wrong. God uses it to help guide and direct us. Teach your children that having a conscience is a wonderful gift. When they have the sense that something's not right—they shouldn't be doing this, or they should stop talking about that—they should be aware that it's their consciences speaking.

You should praise your daughter if she says her conscience bothered her and she stopped or avoided doing something. Or if your son is at a friend's house, a questionable movie is being shown, and his conscience makes him uncomfortable so he leaves, praise him for following his conscience. *"I strive always to keep my conscience clear before God and man"* (Acts 24:16). The more your children learn to listen and follow their consciences, the easier it will be for them to make the right decisions. Help them to develop sensitive consciences by affirming them.

God can use a tender conscience to guide us in what is right and what is wrong. The conscience seems to start as something that is wired into principle and into God's character. But as we exercise it and learn to listen to it, it seems that God's Spirit teams up with it to help us make good decisions. Then it becomes a key in helping us find and follow God's will. However, if we don't listen to the voice of conscience, it becomes less and less sensitive until it becomes what the Bible calls *"seared"* (1 Timothy 4:2). It no longer sends us signals at even the most obvious sins.

c. Quiet Prayer. It's important for you to clarify for your children what prayer is. It isn't that our words swim up through the heavens, to where angels are sitting with fishing lines out, waiting for a nibble before they pull our prayers in, write them down, and put them on God's desk where He will get to them when He has time. God is everywhere. He can have an unlimited number of conversations and, yet, be totally attentive to every one of us.

Teach your children that God is listening to them and is interested in what they have to say. To help them realize this, train them to have a quiet time at the end of their prayers. This is a time of silence: for younger children about thirty seconds, for older children a couple of minutes. Before concluding their prayers, they can ask God if there is anything more He wants them to pray about, any wisdom He wants to give them; and then they wait in silence. *"Be still, and know that I am God"* (Psalm 46:10). For younger children we could give them something to focus on, like thinking about what else to pray for.

This sets a pattern and develops an expectation so that they become used to being quiet before God. This gives God an opportunity to work in their hearts and minds. It's also a way for them to acknowledge and show their confidence that God is real and is interacting with them. It's a powerful statement of belief in God's interest and attention. Children will find that, as they do this, God's presence becomes more and more real to them, and their thoughts get more established and seem to take on a proper order.

d. Peace in Prayer. We can teach our children, when they are praying for something that is important to them, to have specific quiet times for those particular prayers and wait for God to give them peace. They might have to do this for several nights, waiting for peace to come. Jesus said, *"Peace I leave with you; my peace I give you. I do not give to you as the world gives. Do not let your hearts be troubled and do not be afraid"* (John 14:27).

There is a being settled that comes from a right decision when we really commit something to God. This feeling is what we call peace. For example, your son might wonder if he should go to a camp-out. He really wants to go, but every time he prays about it he feels anxious or confused. Then he thinks, "What if I don't go?" He might suddenly start to feel peaceful about it; if this happens, probably God is telling him not to go. You could ask him, "How do you feel about it? When you are quiet in prayer, does it seem like a wise and comfortable decision?" If it doesn't, he could keep on praying and trusting God for wisdom.

Lack of peace doesn't always mean your children shouldn't do something. Occasionally, if God wants them to do difficult things, they might have some resistance; their brains may have difficulty allowing them to have peace. In these cases, encourage them to tell God that they know He knows best and they are willing to do anything He wants them to do. The affirmation of surrender to God's will often clears away the stress. (If you've been a Christian long, you probably can think of examples of this same experience in your own life.)

e. Wisdom. *"If any of you lacks wisdom, he should ask God, who gives generously to all without finding fault, and it will be given to him. But when he asks, he must believe and not doubt, because he who doubts is like a wave of the sea, blown and tossed by the wind. That man should not think he will receive anything from the Lord; he is a double-minded man, unstable in all he does"* (James 1:5–8).

We have to be sure that when we ask God for wisdom we trust Him to give it to us. We must not be double-minded. Teach your children that when they ask God for wisdom, *He will give it to them!* There is no question about it! We know this because of His love and faithfulness.

How will He give your children wisdom? He can use any number of ways. First, He uses the Bible. Second, He works in their hearts and thoughts and just helps them see the issues clearly and make sense of them in light of His principles and character and of what's happening in their lives.

Third, God can also give them wisdom through counsel: godly parents, youth pastor, Sunday School teacher, camp counselor, or others. God can use these people to help your children. With your encouragement, they can learn to go to counselors when they need some additional wisdom. It's important for us to teach them that, ultimately, only God who knows everything can give them the counsel that is right for them; but they can trust Him to speak through the wisdom He has given others.

One thing you need to build into your children solidly is the knowledge that God is all-wise and all-sufficient, and God wants them to know His will. They can be confident that He will make sure they know it; He won't leave them in the dark. So, for example, when they're listening to a counselor speaking and they get that sense of peace, or something the person says hits them with a sense of "this is right," that could be God telling them His will. The more they get to know God and the more sensitive they become to Him, the more easily they'll know when He's giving them His answer.

Ultimately, it all comes back to trust. We read in the Bible that God often led in supernatural ways: angels, visions, talking donkeys, huge fish, and so on. He is very creative. He has a unique relationship with each of us that He will use to lead us; it is up to us to trust Him. God wants us to give Him our lives, seek Him for direction and wisdom, commit to Him daily, and then trust that He's on the job.

God Leads

We need to encourage our children that we don't have to work at finding God's will and plans for us; *He will lead us.* It's difficult for us to define how God leads, because He doesn't follow the same procedure with everyone; nor does He always do it the same way with everyone. If He did, we would soon reduce it to a formula: step one, step two, step three, go. God doesn't do it that way because He wants personal relationships with us.

God is our loving Father, our *Abba,* our Dad; and we're His kids. He wants to lead us more than we want to be led. It's His responsibility to make us aware of His leading and His will. We only need to do what God has asked us to do: trust and commit. We give our lives to God and trust Him; we commit our lives and all our decisions to Him. Then we trust that He will get through to us, using whatever means He needs to do it.

When I (Larry) was a young Christian, God wanted me to leave the business I was a partner in. I was not very open to this at the time, but God got through to me. I was in the business for the wrong reason in the first place. As a non-Christian, my motives were primarily carnal; my sole motivation was to make money. I would not have cheated or deceived people, but my motives were not biblical. For example, I didn't want to maximize my talents or help other people. Once I got saved, I realized that this money motive was wrong, but I still wasn't willing to leave, because I had a lot of time and effort invested in the business. God knew that.

I've never heard God's voice audibly, but I have felt His presence powerfully from time to time in the middle of a decision. God almost always speaks to me through Scripture. As is my habit, I was reading Scripture. I happened to be in the book of Esther.

Mordecai approached Esther about going to see the king in order to plead for the Jews. She didn't want to do it and gave her reason: she could be killed. Mordecai knew that. He said, *"If you remain silent at this time, relief and deliverance for the Jews will arise from another place, but you and your father's family will perish. And who knows but that you have come to royal position for such a time as this?"* (Esther 4:14).

Esther's response was the one that struck a chord in my heart. I'd read this passage before, but God used it this time to speak to me. Esther asked Mordecai to gather people to pray for her. Then she said, *"I will go to the king, even though it is against the law. And if I perish, I perish"* (Esther 4:16).

I realized that right at that moment God was speaking to me and saying, "You must make the decision to obey Me, and the first step is to quit what you're doing. I'm not going to tell you what you're going to do until you quit what you're doing now, because that's the first step of faith and trust." I had never, to my knowledge, trusted God; nor had I ever consciously trusted another human being. I knew God was telling me that He would never be able to use me or show me what to do if I couldn't step out in faith and do this without knowing the next step. So I quit my business.

People have asked how I knew God spoke to me. I like the response Senator Hughes used. He came out of an ornery background, similar to mine. After he became a Christian, someone asked him how he knew he was saved. His reply was one found in Scripture: "All I can tell you is that once I was blind, and now I can see." That's what this situation was like for me. All I can tell you is that I know God was speaking to me. It had never happened before, but without a doubt I knew this was God speaking to me through His Word.

God doesn't speak to everybody in the same way. And He doesn't write us a letter so that we are guaranteed it's Him who is speaking. Yet we can know it is God. But, when we know, we have to be willing to act at once. If we ignore that, it gets more difficult the next time and, eventually, if we keep ignoring God's leading, we won't hear Him speak to us anymore. We can mute His voice, the same as we can sear our consciences.

You can trust God to let your children know what He wants them to do. He wants to lead them and direct them more than they want to be led. The way God chooses to direct them is up to Him. They don't have to be afraid that they'll miss His will. As they commit their lives daily to God and trust Him, He will show them. When He shows them, they mix His answer with faith and trust and follow. For children, God usually will start with smaller things, for example, saying "I'm sorry," but even this can help them to learn to follow His leading.

Persistence, Patience, and Trust

Your children, like you, will discover that, even though you go daily to God, there will be times when it seems like God is not leading or letting you know what to do. You should not get discouraged. *"Who then is the faithful and wise servant, whom the master has put in charge of the servants in his household to give them their food at the proper time? It will be good for that servant whose master finds him doing so when he returns"* (Matthew 24:45–46).

If your kids are trusting God every day, He is fully capable of telling them what He wants them to do. When God seems silent, it's not that "heaven turns to brass"—although it may feel like that. Often what happens is that they are going through rough times. They want things to change, so they start looking for signs that God indeed wants them to do something different. They start thinking, "God, You must want me to change jobs or something." It's really their own lack of contentment that causes them to do this. The clue that they're in danger of doing this is when they start to take on God's responsibilities and think that it's up to them to try to get God's leading instead of simply trusting God to lead them. You should encourage them to relax and let God direct them and change their paths in His own timing.

They should go back to the last thing God told them to do and keep doing it. For example, let's say that Sarah knew she was to go to school and God had provided her with a job selling doughnuts. Now she's halfway through school and doesn't want to sell doughnuts anymore. She might think she needs more money, so she wants to work more hours. She's trying to get God's answer about it—but she doesn't get any answer. Perhaps God knows that the money Sarah is making is enough and that additional hours working will take her away from other priorities. It's easy to start to think that God isn't listening or that He's not on the job, but He is. He just knows that nothing needs to change. Sarah just needs to relax and let Him do His job. She should pray about it but not get anxious. When it's time to change jobs, she will know.

There is nothing wrong with taking our situations to God. The problem comes when we begin to think that it's up to us to change things or to find God's will. Sometimes God tests our faith, but He always has reasons for what He does. Sometimes He'll let us go through things for reasons we can't understand at the time.

In the movie *Karate Kid,* the young hero wanted to learn karate. For weeks his teacher had him painting fences, sanding decks, and polishing cars. The kid got frustrated with this because he could see no purpose for it. How did this manual labor help him learn karate? In reality, his teacher was training him to learn the correct movements and strengthening his arm and leg muscles.

Sometimes God is like this. He takes us down a path and, no matter how we look at it, we can't see how it fits into anything we think God wants us to do. When I (Rick) was first married, my wife and I were praying about what God wanted us to do. We had several options. One of them was selling in a print shop. We prayed about it and felt a real peace about taking this job. So I spent the next couple years learning all there was to know about paper, books, printing, four-color printing, game manufacturing, and so on. In the middle of all this I was trying to figure out what this had to do with anything. What real value did this have? What did it have to do with where I was headed with my life?

I now know that God gave me this job for at least two reasons. First, I met someone through that job who took us into the next stage of what led toward the start of Lightwave. Second, in order to have Lightwave Publishing, I had to know how to build games, deal with artwork and printing materials, and so on. In my first years of starting Lightwave I needed to know everything I had learned at that print shop job. At the time I couldn't see it, but God's direction was very real and extremely practical.

That's why you need to encourage your children not to look too closely and question how this or that thing fits in with their plans or goals. It might not seem to fit their callings or be part of their "career plans." But God always has a purpose. They should look at the seeds of destiny but keep their eyes on God. Sometimes He will take them on roundabout routes to get them where He wants them to go. If He does, they can be sure that there is something God wants them to go through that has a purpose in His plans for them—whether to build character, teach skills, help them gain knowledge they'll need later, or introduce them to people they need to work with.

When God puts us on paths, we should stay on them until He leads to others.

Encourage your children to pray about something before beginning it. Then, when a decision has been made in the right way and they are halfway through their commitment, they should not quit. If, for example, your daughter decided to take violin lessons and halfway through she decided this was not for her, she should be encouraged to finish out that year. Perseverance is a skill and quality that will stand your children in good stead throughout their lives—but only if they learn it.

Remember, God is not in a hurry. He created time. He knows everything that is going on and everything that will happen. God is more in control than you or your children can possibly imagine.

We come back again to trust. Even if things look like a detour, your children can trust God to work it out. He will lead them where He wants them to go—into His wonderful, blessed, gift-filled plan.

Notes

1. If our children don't already know God and have Jesus as their Savior, we need to introduce them to Him. Explain that God loves them very much, and that He gave His Son, Jesus, to die for us so that we could be with God forever. Pray with them when they are ready to accept Jesus as their Savior. Then, when they've given their lives to God assure them that He is faithful.

Once that's established, they need to develop a growing relationship with God and grow in their knowledge of God's Word—His Instruction Manual for Life. Our children also need to have the answers to the big questions: "What is life? Why am I here? How do I find God's purpose for me?" They also need to grow in their understanding of how to seek Him.

We can't cover all of this in this one book. Some other books that deal with these issues are *Talking to Your Children About God* (Harper San Francisco 1998) and *Teaching Your Child How to Pray* (Moody 1997) by Rick Osborne and *Financial Parenting* (Moody 1996) by Larry Burkett and Rick Osborne.

2. See Chapter 2 in *Talking to Your Children About God* by Rick Osborne for practical helps and hints.

1. Teach your children the concept that the way the little things are done today will greatly affect the outcome or the direction of their lives. Do they understand this connection, or are they careless about the "little things" that don't seem to matter?

2. Look in this chapter for the five reasons why God wants to guide us daily. Which of these reasons do you think your children understand best? Which ones don't they understand? Take time to explain the importance and meaning of each reason.

3. What decisions do your children pray about? Point out the ways in which God can speak to them—even in small decisions. Choose a decision they may need to make, explain the steps involved in making decisions, and then talk about the resulting peace from God.

4. Have you ever felt that practical circumstances and God's will sometimes seem to clash? For instance, perhaps you can't afford music lessons for your gifted child. Explain to your children how God uses these circumstances as opportunities for us to seek Him for His provision and direction.

5. Talk to your child about the things he or she is interested in pursuing. How can these pursuits be encouraged to continue? When explaining this issue to your child, relate to an important decision of this nature in your own life to help them understand what you pursued.

6. How does God speak to you in your life? Share examples with your children of different ways God speaks to you, especially through prayer and Scripture. Practice these two disciplines with your children so you can hear from God together.

7. It is hard to measure how persistence, patience, and trust work together to complete our responses to God's plan. Share with your child how this combination worked in a situation in your life when God's will wasn't immediately clear.

Chapter 8

EDUCATION
AND PLANNING

Once we know where God wants us to go, short-term or long-term, we need to start planning how to get there. The question becomes, "How do we plan effectively, following God's will for us, so that we find the calling and place He intended even before we were born?" There's a very good chance that part of what our children will need, to take them to that place, is education and training. And in order to get the right education and training, they will need to have a solid plan in place.

This chapter addresses first the need for education, training, and preparation, and then deals with the planning process.

Education and Training: God's Idea

We have discussed how we need to help our children develop their talents, learn how to round out their personalities, and continue growing in character. These happen in the course of life, but they do require directed training, lessons, education, and practical hands-on experience.

God invented learning, education, and training. You can help your children apply themselves to learning and education because it's a biblical principle. God isn't going to lead them to drop out of school and not get an education. Most of the things that God would call them to will require education.

"*Pay attention and listen to the sayings of the wise; apply your heart to what I teach*" (Proverbs 22:17). "*Apply your heart to instruction and your ears to words of knowledge*" (Proverbs 23:12). "*Buy the truth and do not sell it; get wisdom, discipline and understanding*" (Proverbs 23:23).

Among the best educated people in the Bible were Daniel and his friends, Shadrach, Meshach, and Abed-nego. They decided to put God first by not eating the Babylonian food that was against God's Law to eat. The result was that they were healthier than those who had enjoyed the rich Babylonian food and wine. And, as a result of their obedience to God and their commitment to excellence, "*To these four young men God gave knowledge and understanding of all kinds of literature and learning. . . . The king talked with them, and he found none equal to [them]. . . . In every matter of wisdom and understanding about which the king questioned them, he found them ten times better than all the magicians and enchanters in his whole kingdom*" (Daniel 1:17, 19–20).

As Christians we sometimes have the idea that, because our kids are Christians, it's all right to put less emphasis on education and academics, because they have more important priorities in life. Some Christian schools don't push academics but spend more time on Bible training. We shouldn't have to sacrifice one for the other. Both are important.

Daniel and company had their eyes focused on God and kept Him first in their lives. Yet they still applied themselves to their studies and strove for excellence in all areas. This is an example you should encourage your children to follow. They should keep their eyes and ears focused on God, especially in the middle of today's secular educational system. With this focus they should be able to excel, because God will give them wisdom. "*The fear of the Lord is the beginning of knowledge, but fools despise wisdom and discipline*" (Proverbs 1:7).

This attitude of God first, and of naturally involving God in their learning, is something that they can get hold of from a young age. Encourage your children to pray about their education all along the way, from learning how to spell and count, through social studies and calculus, and on to a college or university. Then they can apply this habit of praying, as a matter of course, to studying and learning of every type and at every level.

Be Flexible

Education is God's idea. It is His will for children. He wants to share the wonders and intricacies of His world with them. But in this day and age the educational opportunities are so varied that it is sometimes difficult for children to decide what to pursue and where. How can they know what education and training they need?

If they are going to be doctors, pharmacists, teachers, or whatever, they will need the education that will equip them for the task. Postsecondary education is becoming an increasing need in our changing world. The 350 million workers in the industrialized countries, whose pay averages $18 an hour, are suddenly competing with the 1.2 billion workers in developing nations whose wages average less than $2 an hour! As a result, the majority of unskilled labor has been exported.

This has created a situation in which at least some postsecondary education is required if one hopes to achieve a comfortable, middle-class lifestyle. Generally speaking, twenty-first century workers will more likely have to be generalists who have specialist capabilities; a college education will give them the basic capabilities they will need.

However, we should be cautious in pushing our children toward a university or college education. We need to be flexible and help them see *all* the options that are available. God's path for them may not be the conventional one. They might feel that God is telling them to do something that does not require a degree.

For example, your son may feel that God wants him to be a professional snowboarder. Chances are good that he won't need a lot of postsecondary education to learn how to snowboard. Alternatively, if he's going to be a championship snowboarder, he might end up getting endorsement contracts and so on. For that he will need to understand business principles.

Or what if your daughter feels God wants her to do something that doesn't require a four-year college or university degree, but for some reason she feels that God wants her to go to the university and get that degree anyway?

When our children pray through their plans, it might not make absolutely logical sense. Generally it should, but sometimes God will lead them to do things that, to our commonsense minds, don't make sense. Whatever they are being led into, we need to stand behind them and encourage them as they check out their options. We also need to help them strive consistently for excellence in all they do.

Excellence and Honor

It's important that we help our children get the basic education, develop their personalities and talents, learn life skills, and grow in character. We also need to help them get the relevant education and/or training for the particular areas they are preparing to enter.

Education takes them only so far; then training is needed. Let's say your son is musically inclined and wants to be involved in production, making the music sound absolutely fantastic on tape. He can get all kinds of education about music, sound theory, and production, but if he walks into a studio and says, "I have a degree. I'd like a job," the chances are good that he will be handed a broom and told, "Start sweeping the floors; then you might be able to work your way up." The expectation of being able to walk into a high-level, high-paying job just by asking will be disappointing. Your son should understand the need to apprentice and gain experience.

In days gone by, young children, usually boys, would be apprenticed to a master. They would spend their lives learning to be carpenters, smiths, artists, or whatever. They would get knowledge from their masters and have lots of hands-on, practical training as well. Today we see this dedication and apprenticeship to some degree with Olympic athletes and figure skaters. But most kids are taught a smattering of a variety of things and have the attitude that as long as they know enough to get by, they'll be fine.

Or kids might have the get-rich-quick, fast-food, fast-everything mentality. We have lost the art of valuing craftsmanship, expertise, and excellence. We no longer take the time to do something right and to the very best of our abilities. Appliances are made to last a few years so that people will have to buy new ones. This whole cultural attitude makes it easy for our children to lose sight of the benefits of doing things *really* well.

However, in contrast to the attitude of our society, the reality is that if our children learn to develop their talents to excellence, they will succeed and be respected. If they love to learn, if they develop their brains, and if they trust God in the whole process, they will be able to make a significant difference in the world. They will have an impact on their communities and on the lives of those around them.

It's not about making money, although when people develop their talents like this, they are rewarded. *"Do you see a man skilled in his work? He will serve before kings; he will not serve before obscure men"* (Proverbs 22:29). When our children see themselves as unimportant, they may feel that all they can do is find their little spot, make enough money to be comfortable, and look after themselves. But when they understand that God has significant places for them, they will know that they matter and can make a difference in the world. They will realize it's about finding their unique spots in history and making their own special contributions to society.

The key is for us to push our children to excel in *all* the things God gave them. They have a contribution to make to their world. We should instill in them the confidence that, as they develop to excellence in who God made them to be, He will take them far beyond what they think they are able to do. They need to *know* that God can give them wisdom beyond their wildest dreams. He's designed them for noble purposes. He will help them find and fulfill those purposes as they trust Him, commit their way to Him, and follow Him.

As they follow this God-ordained process, they will find themselves being honored in their fields and in their communities. In turn, this reflects on God and shows the world that He is a loving, wonderful, trustworthy God.

Look at George Washington Carver. His education was hard-won, but he constantly went to God for help. One day he asked God to reveal the secrets of the universe to him. God said, "No. But I'll reveal the secrets of the peanut to you." And He did. Through the years that followed, Carver discovered hundreds of uses for peanuts and developed a myriad of products from them and from sweet potatoes—to such an extent that his work helped to change the whole economy of the southern United States. He literally was brought before the rulers of the land, before presidents and statesmen—all because he went to God, trusted God to guide him, and excelled in his field.

This is exactly what happened to Daniel, Shadrach, Meshach, and Abed-nego as well. They trusted God and refused to compromise their faith. They remained focused on God, deciding to serve God and put Him first. God gave them wisdom in every discipline and area of study known at the time. So when the king tested them, their answers were superior to those of every other knowledgeable person in the kingdom. God did not just wave His magic wand and suddenly they were wise. They worked for it, applied themselves, and trusted God to cause them to excel. As a result, all of them held high positions in the land. They were a testimony to God that even the king recognized and acknowledged.

Love to Learn

As we encourage our children to excellence, we also need to instill in them a love of learning. Learning is not a necessary evil; it is wonderful and exciting, full of adventure and surprising gems, like a treasure chest found unexpectedly. We can teach our children that God wants them to learn, that they can excel at learning, that it's fun, and that they can learn all kinds of things—like Daniel and his friends.

You can help *make* learning fun by showing your kids when they are very young that they can learn. When they learn anything, you can praise them for it and make it an exciting accomplishment. Applaud them with statements like, "Wow! Look what you just learned! You're good at learning." Always encourage them in their ability to learn, but never tell them that they are stupid or make them feel they are slow or dumb. By helping them trust God and believe that they can learn, and by helping them love the process of learning, they will excel.

I (Larry) never had a love of learning instilled in me. I didn't know it was important, so in school I did what I needed to do to get by, but I never really studied or did my best. I had decided at a young age that I would get a college education, but it had never clicked that I would need good grades to do that. When the time came to think about college, I discovered that because my grades were not great, scholarships were out of the question. And financially I couldn't do it on my own. So I decided to enter the military and get training through them.

I shared my plans with a teacher of mine, and he was enthusiastic. But he told me before I joined the armed services that I needed to *learn how to learn.* That is the first time I remember an adult consciously sitting down and talking to me like I was an adult. He said, "You know, Larry, I can see that you can grasp these concepts; the problem is you just don't ever want to. Unless you learn to concentrate and take the time to learn, you'll never go anywhere. I don't care how good your mind is. If you want to go to college, you're going to have to study." This was a radical new concept for me. I had never been taught about learning.

I had many teachers who believed in me. Even back in grammar school, when I was doing poorly, teachers would call me in after class and say, "You know, you've got the brains, you just don't have the skills." And I remember that I used to laugh about it. They believed that I could do it, but none of them cared enough to make it happen. But Mr. Blackwelder did. He taught me to learn, and that changed the direction of my whole life, because from that time on I began to apply myself and excel in whatever the subject was.

If parents don't take the time, or somebody else doesn't take the time, to explain things to children, to teach them the need to learn, to help them love learning and believe they can do it, how will they know? Without this, school, studying, and learning will be difficult chores or simply necessary evils.

Praying or Planning?

Getting a relevant education and training involves planning. Planning does not contradict God's leading. He designed it.

There seems to be an idea among some Christians that we can either be led by God's Spirit or plan and map out our own lives. This approach sees praying and planning as mutually exclusive: If you follow God you don't need to plan, and if you plan you don't need to consult God. That's just not the way it is. The Bible teaches us to do *both.* It encourages us to plan but to submit the planning process to God and to bathe all our planning in prayer. Sometimes this means not going with what common sense dictates. We can't just set up a plan based on common sense and say it has to work this way.

Even though God's leading does not always take us to places that "make sense," God is not against planning. He is for it. He invented it. God came up with the idea of planning; it's part of how He designed things to work, and it's an integral part of how we find His will. We need to be careful not to plan without prayer or to pray without planning.

True biblical planning is Spirit-led-and-if-the-Lord-wills planning. *"Now listen, you who say, 'Today or tomorrow we will go to this or that city, spend a year there, carry on business and make money.' Why, you do not even know what will happen tomorrow. What is your life? You are a mist that appears for a little while and then vanishes. Instead, you ought to say, 'If it is the Lord's will, we will live and do this or that'"* (James 4:13–15).

Notice that James does not condemn planning—only planning without God's input. This means we should submit our plans to God from the beginning and all along the way. There are many examples in the Bible that show us this process.

In Egypt, God gave Joseph the plan for saving Egypt from the coming famine by storing grain from the years of bountiful crops. Joseph was put in charge of implementing this plan. He didn't just keep praying for seven years that somehow God would keep the famine from happening. He had to put feet to a clear plan and put it into action city by city. He built storehouses, assigned supervisors, and tallied up the grain going into the storehouses. He had to decide, when the famine arrived, how they were going to give it out, what they would charge, and so on.

This was an enormous plan that needed someone with Joseph's unique talents. God had trained Joseph for many years for this task. The plan worked so well, and Egypt gathered so much grain, that Joseph stopped keeping inventory. Egypt gained great wealth as a result of Joseph's selling the grain to those from other nations who came for food.

David knew that God wanted a temple to be built, but God told him he couldn't build it but that he could plan and get ready for it. So he made an incredible, detailed plan for the temple. He planned it and then prepared and collected all the materials his son Solomon would need to build the temple.

Nehemiah heard that the walls of Jerusalem were broken down. He asked the king of Babylon if he could go and investigate the situation. When he arrived, he took a close look at the state of the walls. They were so bad, he wept. He knew that he was the one God had appointed to repair the damage. So, with prayer, he set the goal that God gave him: to repair the walls. Then he put together a plan to accomplish that goal.

There are numerous other examples throughout the Bible of how God gave a goal to someone and then that person carried it out. God appointed the apostle Paul to preach to the Gentiles. Paul knew that was his calling and set about accomplishing the task. He went from city to city spreading the news. At every stage he prayed about where to go next.

We know he planned ahead because of comments in his letters that indicate that he had planned to visit certain areas, but God sent him in a different direction or he was prevented from carrying out his plan (see Acts 16:6–10). *"I planned many times to come to you (but have been prevented from doing so until now)"* (Romans 1:13). *"Since I have been longing for many years to see you, I plan to do so when I go to Spain. I hope to visit you while passing through"* (Romans 15:23–24).

From this it is clear that planning and being led by God's Spirit are not contradictory; they are complementary. But the key is to plan the right thing—what God has called us to do. So first, as discussed in the previous chapter, we need to determine what God has called us to do. Once we have that goal, God doesn't leave us to our own devices. All through the planning process and the implementation of that plan, He is with us as we continue to pray and seek His wisdom and direction. He wants to be involved in our plans as a loving, caring Father.

If we make a list of the stages of planning, we will not find prayer as *one* of the steps: It permeates every single step. It must be a part of every stage of planning. Your children can begin learning this at a very young age. You can teach them to pray about each stage of a plan as they develop their talents and gifts.

Suppose your daughter is very kinesthetic and musical. She might want to join a baseball team, a soccer team, and a ballet class, but she also wants to take violin and voice. She might want to go with all her desires. You'll need to sit down with her at an age when she can think this through, and you walk her through the process. You can ask her what her talents are and what she wants to do. If she took piano lessons last year and now she wants to take violin, you might ask her to consider developing her piano skills to a certain level of expertise. You can encourage her to pray about it and consider the wise plan for developing her talents rather than using the shotgun approach, which gives her a smattering of everything but skill in little.

If you teach your children to plan things in an atmosphere of prayer, you'll be surprised at what they will come up with. However, if you allow them to jump from thing to thing, simply going with what they feel like doing, they will make decisions about college and classes the same way when the time comes. When you teach them to plan in small ways, it will give them skills and habits of prayer that will carry over into the big decisions.

As they implement their plan, they may find that things have to change as they meet circumstances they didn't anticipate. At that point they need to continue to involve God and seek His guidance. They shouldn't abandon the plan, but they need to be open to adapting it.

There's a young man who believes that God has called him to full-time ministry. His plan involves getting a theological degree at a seminary. During seminary, he attends and helps in a local church. After seminary, he plans to seek a position as an assistant pastor and eventually become a senior pastor. But in his final year at seminary, the pastor of the local church he is attending resigns or retires. The board is so pleased with this young man's work in the church for the past couple of years that they ask him to consider taking on the pastorate. They tell him he has been so faithful that they are willing to provide an assistant while he finishes his degree, and then they want him to take over as senior pastor. That wasn't in his plan.

It would be foolish of him to say, "Oh no! I'm going to finish my degree then be an assistant pastor." Rather, he should pray about it. It is possible that this was God's plan all along, only the young man had no way of foreseeing this when he prayed and laid out his plan.

Or, take a younger child who is very artistic. Her plan is to major in art in high school and then go on to an art college. She has, in her high school, a great art teacher, who is able to teach the basics in an excellent, easy-to-understand way. She encourages the girl and is successfully helping her to establish the basic skills she will need to get into the college of her choice.

Then, when this girl is halfway through high school, the art teacher leaves. The replacement teacher, however, is not as good and isn't able to teach the girl the basic skills she needs. She has to take another look at her plan, so she prays about it. Instead of getting discouraged or changing her plan for art college, she feels that God may be directing her to change high schools and attend a school that has an excellent art program. With that kind of prayer bathing her decision, she likely will find herself in a situation in which she excels even more and is even better prepared for college.

We need to keep our plans flexible, especially when we see that something has changed. But this doesn't mean, if your son has set a three-year goal for a particular level of skill at playing the piano but halfway through decides he's sick of it, that he should quit. That's not a good reason to change the plan. If he prayed about his plan at the beginning, he should stick with it.

All of this goes along with what we discussed in the previous chapter about following God's will and being sensitive to the Holy Spirit's leading. This is true at every one of the six stages of the planning process.

The Six-Stage Planning Process

The following is a planning process you can use to teach your children, as soon as they are old enough to understand it. It can apply to any planning needed, from the simplest to the most complicated scenarios, so it is something children can use throughout their lives. We have provided, at the end of the chapter, a template that you can use to guide your children through this process. There are spaces allotted to each stage mentioned below. You might want to photocopy and/or enlarge several copies of the template so your children can investigate a variety of options. This practical tool can help to make the process easy and ordinary for your children.

1. Inventory the Seeds of Destiny: Make an list of the various seeds of destiny, such as personality type and talents. Help your children write on a piece of paper the various things they have learned about themselves that we have discussed in this book.

- **Personality type**—Your child can write his or her personality type, as determined by the survey mentioned in Chapter 3 and provided in the Appendix. This should include the two highest scores. For example, high D, high I, in which high D is the highest score and high I is the second-highest. Note the strengths of that personality type (both for the highest and the second-highest scores), especially those that they relate to the most.
- **Talents and gifts**—Then your child can note his or her talents and gifts, as perceived by himself or herself and by others. You may need to help with this. It may help to divide talents and gifts into primary and secondary. Your child will be stronger in some and less strong in others. The list should be as long as possible. Younger children may have gifts that are as yet undeveloped and seem small now but may be a key to God's plan.
- **Likes and wants**—Children should also write their desires: what they want to do, what they see themselves doing, and what they like doing now.
- **Seeds of destiny**—Any "seeds of destiny" can be written. Is there something inside your child that says, "I really want to do this one thing"? This also may include a special event or opportunity that has influenced or cultivated a desire to go in a certain direction.
- **Peace**—This is the place to note things he or she has a peace about and has sensed any kind of direction from God on, as discussed in Chapter 7. If this hasn't happened yet, that's fine; it will come at some point in the planning process. Take this opportunity, though, to encourage your child to begin to pray for God's wisdom and direction.

Help your children through the process by asking them relevant questions to get them thinking. For example, ask them what they feel they are good at, what things people have told them they do well, and so on. Once they have it written down, help them see the patterns in it. Discuss the seeds of destiny with them, helping them see where they point. Remember to be objective.

Don't force something you think of into the list, and don't draw conclusions that aren't really supported by the list. Instead, if you understand the material covered in this book, you should be able to help your child come up with and write down the information and then encourage him or her to see patterns or directions in which the seeds of destiny could be pointing.

To help clarify the process we have filled out one sheet for you with a hypothetical example of a boy called Jamie. It is on the following page.

When we step back and look at these seeds of destiny we can see that they are possibly pointing Jamie in the direction of competitive snowboarding or law. Your child's inventory may not be as conclusive as this, but you should be able to see one or more strong patterns emerging. As you discuss these patterns and have your child pray further about it, clarity will come in time. Updating or redoing the survey as your children grow older is a wise idea.

2. Investigate: *On the basis of the inventory, list job or career possibilities and investigate the ones that are of greatest interest.*

After seeing where your children's seeds of destiny point and listing a few possibilities of what they might be pointing toward, it's time to investigate the options. Teach your children to investigate options, job markets, business opportunities, education requirements, and financial needs. You also can help them learn how to look into the areas they are interested in.

JAMIE'S INVENTORY

Personality Type: High I and High D: *Influencing* and *Dominant*

Strengths:

Influencing: Driven naturally to relate to others; verbal, friendly, outgoing, and optimistic; typically enthusiastic motivator and will seek others to help; function best in a friendly environment.

Dominant: Naturally motivated to control his environment; assertive, direct, and strong-willed; typically bold and not afraid to take strong action to get the desired results; function best in a challenging environment.

Other: I'm a good showman; I enjoy people and am friendly. I can think in business terms. I am a leader.

Primary Talents and Gifts: I'm good at sports, especially snowboarding. I've already won some competitions and people have told me I could really go far with it. I love thrills and the competition and I don't get nervous.

Secondary Talents and Gifts: I'm smart and I can think quickly on my feet. I love seeing the big picture and putting pieces of puzzles together. I love figuring things out and solving problems.

What I Want To Do: I want to compete and be a professional in snowboarding. I love competing, and I love the thrill of "me against the mountain." I also love the idea of the law and helping people with legal problems. I'd love to be a lawyer.

My Seed of Destiny: Ever since almost my first time on a snowboard I've known that this is what I want to do. It's just perfect for me. I've always known that I would compete in an area of sports and do really well. My uncle is a lawyer, and every time he's around I can't seem to stop asking him questions. When I hear him talk, it seems like I would love doing everything he does.

God's Leading and Peace: I've prayed about snowboarding professionally, and I feel really peaceful about it. But I also think maybe I should be a lawyer, and that seems okay when I pray about it too.

Other Options I've Thought Of: Being in business for myself; skiing pro.

These all seem quite pragmatic and even secular; but, remember that God created planning and common sense. He also knew all of these factors when He mapped out a plan for our children's lives. Although these steps cannot replace God's leading, they are important and can be seeds of destiny to God's direction. First, help them list the things they need to find out; then help them investigate and write their conclusions.

Let's go back to Jamie.

JAMIE'S INVESTIGATION

The areas my seeds of destiny are pointing toward and that I'm going to pray about and investigate: competitive snowboarding and law

The first area: competitive snowboarding

What I need to find out: How do I become a professional snowboarder? How many years can a snowboarding career last? After snowboarding, how likely is it that I'll be able to be a coach or an instructor? Or could I go into a snowboarding business of some sort? What kind of income will it provide?

What I found out: I become professional by entering and winning competitions. Snowboarding careers only last five to ten years. What I can do afterward depends on how well I do and how well-known in the field I become. The demand for coaches or instructors isn't great, but it's a growing area. In a few years there might be more jobs. It's the same with selling snowboards, so it might be hard to get a job in the field after I stop competing. But if I do really well, I could get some contracts for endorsing products. The income depends on what competitions I win.

The second area: law

What I need to find out: How long will it take to become a lawyer? How much does it cost? Where are the main, well-respected law schools? What about how long a law career lasts? What grades and other prerequisites are required to go to law school?

What I found out: I need a university degree before going to law school. It's expensive. There's a great law school in the nearest city, and a law career can last as long as I want it to.

154 ◆ YOUR CHILD WONDERFULLY MADE

Jamie won't make a decision based on income, but it is a consideration. Since snowboarding careers don't last that long, Jamie decides he will need to do something afterward. He thinks he could go into law after his snowboarding career ends.

3. *Explore:* *Get a hands-on feel for the job(s) or profession(s) that resulted from the investigation.*

In this stage your children should get a hands-on feel for the profession. Encourage them to find out what the job actually entails from people working in that field. And remind them to pray while they are there.

Often in the exploration your children will discover something they didn't realize was involved. This discovery process can help alleviate their doubts, get more information that confirms their desires, or it might even change it. By being there at "ground zero," they can get a sense of whether this really is something they want to pursue.

JAMIE'S EXPLORATION

What I'm exploring: snowboarding/law

What I can do: I can talk to a professional snowboarder at the mountain where I snowboard. I know someone who can introduce me to one. I can visit a courtroom and watch lawyers at work. I can get books out of the library on snowboarding and on law. I can search the Internet. I can try to talk to a lawyer. I'll talk to my uncle about being a lawyer and see if I can visit his office.

What I found out: There really is a chance to go far with snowboarding. I've already won more competitions than the guy I talked to had at my age, but there are more competitions around now. He trains all winter and has a training program in the summer. He knows some coaches who might take me on. But I found out, as I sat in court and prayed about it, that I don't want to argue criminal law in court. I also discovered that there are all kinds of lawyers, and some of them rarely see the inside of a courtroom. There's such a thing as a lawyer who specializes in sports! I could do that!

These second and third stages can begin when your children are still quite young. For example, your young daughter might decide she wants to be a dentist. The next time you take her to see the dentist, you could phone ahead and ask if the dentist can spend a few minutes at the end of your visit talking to her about what his job is like.

Your young children's desires and likes will probably change frequently. But if you teach them to investigate and explore options in this way, they will have this skill and habit when they really need it. Remember to always accompany exploration with prayer.

4. Set goals: *After the first three steps have been settled, what are the specific goals I want to reach? What do I want to be doing? by when?*

When your children are younger, they probably will go through the previous steps several times. As they get older and narrow down the options, they can go on to this stage. Now they will have a pretty clear idea where they want to go. They believe they know what God wants them to do. It's time to get specific and make specific goals that are measurable—what they want to be doing and by when.

Make your children aware that some of these goals might change as they go into actual step-by-step planning and find out more details.

JAMIE'S GOALS

What I want to do: I will be a competitive and professional snowboarder. Then, when that career is over I will be a lawyer who specializes in the area of sports.

When I will do this: I will turn professional right after I graduate from high school. I will enter six main competitions in my first season and then more each year. I will be in the national competitions within four years. I will have passed my bar exam by the time I'm 30 and will be established in my law career by the time I'm 35.

5. Plan: *Put together a plan that will help you achieve the goals set in step 4.*

The time has come to put things together. This stage involves more investigation. Teach your children the skill of researching, whether it be through the Internet, the library, or the telephone. They should be able to call a university and ask about courses and request information and so on. Don't be tempted to do too much for your kids. You can do some and show them what you're doing. Then explain the process to them and then leave them to do it alone, with your support, in case they run into problems. You won't always be around to do it for them; it's a life skill they need to learn.

Each stage takes us deeper and deeper into the planning process. And each step is a bit more difficult and involved. But because you are taking your children through it one step at a time and teaching them the basic skills for each stage, beginning when they're young, it won't be overwhelming when they come to big decisions.

JAMIE'S PLAN

The places I can study/compete: There are competitions locally that will give me a good start. Then I'll have to start competing regionally and, eventually, nationally. If I do well there, I can go international! The university runs through the winter, during my peak snowboarding time. There are a couple universities that run on a semester program, so I could take some courses in the summer. I have to finish the university; then I'll go to law school. That means it'll be about seven years before my bar exam.

The courses and grades I will need in high school: My grades are good enough, but I have to keep them up if I want to go to law school, so I'll have to maintain a good grade average at the university too.

What I found out about the education or training I need: I can take university courses in the summer, but that means it will take longer to finish than I thought. I will need to really focus on my snowboarding and train hard if I'm going to succeed. Because it will take me longer to reach my law goal, I'll take my bar exam later.

And all along the way they should be praying through their planning and not putting anything on paper without God's input. They should be asking God to help them gather the right information and to open the right doors for them. God will give them wisdom to know how to set their discoveries and plans on paper.

So they have their plan. Their goals are right and fit the plan. They've found a way to put it all together.

Jamie has found a way to do his first years of university and his snowboarding at the same time. After that he'll go to law school. His snowboarding career will have peaked, and if he does well enough he'll be signing some endorsement contracts on the side to help finance law school. Everything matches with his inventory and the things he's discovered. His plans take him to his goals, and, most important, he has a real peace about it all.

6. Finances: *Put together a financial plan.*

The final step of planning is the nitty-gritty of finances. As your children look into the financial aspect of things, they'll find that it will change things once again. It's important to be sure that your children have their priorities right. They can, first of all, trust God to take care of them and meet their needs. He will help them to get through their education. But God also wants them to be able to work and provide for themselves and those who depend on them.

In addition, God wants us to be giving back out of what we have to our churches and communities, so you should help your children build good stewardship and wise money handling into their lives and plans. For a lot more information and practical help, see our book, *Financial Parenting,* published by Moody Press.

Jamie may have to change his plans. If he puts all his resources down on paper and finds he can't make it, he may have to just snowboard and wait to attend the university and law school. It looks like it might take him a few years longer to reach his goal. However, if he does really well in his snowboarding, there will be endorsements and other contracts that will provide money for the university and law school. With some additional prayer and with God's help he might find other sources for funds along the way, such as other scholarships, sponsorships, and so on.

JAMIE'S FINANCES

Cost of my education: The university will cost $_____ a year, full-time, or $_____ a semester. For four years that means $_____, if I live at home rather than on campus. Snowboarding equipment for a year will cost $_____. Entrance fees for the competitions I need to enter will cost $_____. Coaches fees will cost $_____. Living and spending money while living at home will be $_____ per month.

My financial resources: I have $_____ in my savings that I've put away. My folks have $_____ saved for me toward my college education.

Other sources of money: I can get an athletic and maybe even an academic scholarship to the university I want to go to that is worth $_____. I can get sponsored for snowboarding for $_____ a competition and $_____ for equipment. I can work_____ hours a week without it interfering with my training. I can get a job on the mountain in the winter and make $_____ a season. Out of that I will be able to put $_____ in the bank. I can win prize money from competitions that could be worth $_____, but I can't count on this. If I win the top contest I could win a prize of $100,000! That would go a long way!

My shortfall or excess: I'll be okay for snowboarding and I'll be able to put a bit in the bank, and I'll be okay for the university. But I won't have enough to attend law school without some prize money. That means I should carefully save any and all prize money or endorsement money I earn.

You don't want your kids to say, "The finances aren't here. I can't make it work. I guess I shouldn't do it." Instead, if they are sure that this is what God wants them to do, you should remind them that God can be trusted to work out the finances. They can keep on investigating and going forward. They may have to get started without everything being in place, but they will just need to take it one step at a time and trust in God. He will be faithful in providing for them, as long as they are doing the best they can.

Suppose Jamie were your son. And let's say he got a summer job making more money than he expected. Instead of going off and spending it on a trip to the Swiss Alps, he should put it toward his plan—put it in the bank and save it for law school.

Your children's plans need to be flexible and based on prayer. God looked forward and saw every detail of your children's lives, including family, people, education, money, and every circumstance and situation. Then He designed them specifically to fit their situations and this time in a unique and special way. Now they can look, from their end, at who they are, who God made them to be, and what He has given to them. From that knowledge, with prayer, they can then discover the way forward, the way through the world around them.

Stewards or Owners?

It's interesting to note that according to a recent Gallup poll, only 50 percent of young people said their parents or family had a higher degree of influence in their lives than anyone else. Friends ranked as the number one influence on young people (87 percent). And religion came in below music, movies, and television at only 13 percent.[1]

As parents, we need to work hard to retrieve our influence over our children. We need to faithfully teach, encourage, and guide them. But when we make decisions for them and push them, we misuse our influence and start to lose it. Biblically speaking, parents have been given a special trust to serve as stewards or managers of their children. Unfortunately, some parents view their role as *owners* rather than stewards, an attitude that causes many problems and conflicts.

We must ask ourselves: Do I view myself as an owner or a steward? If we realize that we see ourselves as owners, we'll likely feel responsible for what our children will do as adults, and we will apply pressure to mold them into the careers we think they should follow. But as stewards we are concerned only with helping them develop and grow into God's plans for them, through sound guidance and encouragement. With this kind of help, they can become what God has equipped them to be.

It is difficult to detect an attitude of ownership, because the differences between ownership and stewardship are subtle. Our first clue will be that we find ourselves trying to control their occupational choices. Many parents struggle with being good stewards, especially if their child's bent is different from theirs or different from what they would like it to be. But our focus of loving guidance and support is essential.

Psychologists who study children's development agree that bonding with their caregivers, whether parents or someone else, is crucial for a normal childhood—as crucial as learning to walk or talk.

Love, support, and encouragement never cease to be the most powerful parental tools, and they will always keep your children coming back to you for more help and advice.

Note

1 "America's Youth in the 90s." Princeton: The George H. Gallup International Institute, 1993.

INVENTORY OF SEEDS OF DESTINY

Personality type: _____

Strengths: _____

_____

_____

_____

_____

Primary talents and gifts (what I'm good at and what people have noticed I do well): _____

_____

_____

_____

_____

Secondary talents and gifts (what I'm good at but not as strong in): ___

_____

_____

_____

_____

What I want to do: _____

_____

_____

_____

My seeds of destiny: _____

_____

_____

God's leading and peace: _____

_____

_____

_____

INVESTIGATION

The areas my seeds of destiny point toward and that I'm going to pray about and investigate: _____

_____

_____

The first area: _____

What I need to find out: _____

_____

_____

What I found out: _____

_____

_____

_____

_____

The second area: _____

What I need to find out: _____

_____

_____

What I found out: _____

_____

_____

_____

_____

_____

EXPLORATION

The area I'm exploring: _____

What I can do to explore it: _____

_____

_____

_____

_____

What I found out: _____

_____

_____

_____

_____

GOALS

What I want to do: _____

_____

_____

_____

_____

When I will do this: _____

_____

_____

MY PLAN

The places I can study: _____

_____

_____

_____

The courses and grades I will need in high school: _____

_____

_____

_____

The education or training I will need: _____

_____

_____

_____

_____

_____

_____

_____

_____

MY FINANCES

My education will cost:_____

_____

_____

_____

My financial resources: _____

_____

_____

_____

_____

_____

I can get other money from: _____

_____

_____

_____

_____

_____

My shortfall or excess: _____

_____

_____

_____

_____

Part 3

A HIGHER CALLING

"Lead me in the way everlasting"
(Psalm 139:24).

Chapter 9

THE HOPE
OF HEAVEN

In the church in our western culture today, we are seeing an emphasis on God's love for us, His desire to care for us and be an intimate part of our lives, and the fact that He wants the best for us. These things have been discussed at length in this book. It is all very true. God does want to be our loving Father and to do for us all the things the best fathers do.

But this is not the whole story. What we need to remember and instill in our children is that God did not make us just for this life; He made us with eternity in mind. If we look at all the signposts of our lives, we see that they point us toward our ultimate calling here on Earth. But as Christians our ultimate destiny is really eternity with God in heaven. Our lives here are merely drops in the bucket in comparison to the big picture. This life is simply preparation for the real thing—like preschool or kindergarten are places to get your children ready for school.

The future is foretold clearly in the Bible, from Abraham to the apostle John. Hebrews tell us that Abraham *"was looking forward to the city with foundations, whose architect and builder is God"* (Hebrews 11:10).

He looked forward to eternity with God. In the New Testament we are told repeatedly that our hope as Christians is our eternity with God. It is that awesome and wonderful privilege and blessing that God has prepared for us. He is making a place in eternity where *"He will wipe every tear from their eyes. There will be no more death or mourning or crying or pain"* (Revelation 21:4).

God created us with all our idiosyncrasies, uniqueness, and individualities. He created talents, abilities, plans, goals, and achievements. He didn't do all of this just for us to use now. When we reach heaven, we will not do and be totally different people than we are now. This life is not a waste that is cast aside once it is over, as if it were trash. All that we are, all we have known, learned, and experienced, is not done away with as useless and valueless. It is a seed, a starting place. Things go on from here to something built on what we do here—but much, much better. To put it colloquially, we ain't seen nothin' yet!

"How great is the love the Father has lavished on us, that we should be called children of God! And that is what we are! The reason the world does not know us is that it did not know him. Dear friends, now we are children of God, and what we will be has not yet been made known. But we know that when he appears, we shall be like him, for we shall see him as he is. Everyone who has this hope in him purifies himself, just as he is pure" (1 John 3:1–3).

If when we see Him we will be completely purified in an instant, why do we need to continually purify ourselves now? There is a connection between who we will be in heaven and who we are now.

"So will it be with the resurrection of the dead. The body that is sown is perishable, it is raised imperishable; it is sown in dishonor, it is raised in glory; it is sown in weakness, it is raised in power; it is sown a natural body, it is raised a spiritual body. . . . For the perishable must clothe itself with the imperishable, and the mortal with immortality" (1 Corinthians 15:42–44, 53).

In the verses before this Paul talks about our mortal body here on Earth being like a seed compared to how we will be in heaven. Who we are in heaven comes out of who we are here, but we are much better.

We don't know for sure what we will be like or what heaven will be like. We do know that it will be more fantastic than we can imagine. When God created Adam and Eve He created them, and through them all people, with the intent that we would be with Him forever and be His children throughout eternity. We probably will be like babies again in the context of how much growing and learning we'll have to do. But the preparation we've done here, the things we've learned, the talents He's given us that we develop, are seeds that will be used in heaven too.

The way God created us to be and the calling He's given us here must all be in preparation for heaven. How He made us is not going to change in a night. We are who He intentionally designed us to be, with both now and eternity in mind. So we are going on to even greater and more wonderful things in heaven—things that fit us and suit us perfectly. God has things for us to do in heaven that match who He created us to be.

When your children are planning for this life—what they will do, who they will marry, how many kids they'll have, and so on—you need to make sure they know that their hope is eternity. Without this knowledge, it is easy for them to get caught up in the things that happen down here and to consider making choices based on what will give them the best possible life here and now. However, if they are eternity-minded and heaven-focused, when a right and wrong choice comes up and doing the wrong thing will propel them forward here, like Moses, they will choose God's way instead of enjoying sin for a time.

It's important for you to read to your children about heaven and how wonderful it will be. It's great fun to tell them about the new glorified bodies they will have. This stimulates their imagination and gets them looking forward to heaven as an exciting place to be. We need to encourage them with the hope and joy of heaven.

Our Places in History

We are not citizens here; we are citizens of heaven. Here we are strangers, ambassadors for God to a world that desperately needs hope and the knowledge of a loving God. We need to teach our children the significance of *when* God has placed us in history. We are living in the time when Jesus Christ has come and given His life for the world. He left here telling us that, between that time and His return, we need to go and tell everyone about the opportunity to be in a restored relationship with God. We need to tell them of the privilege of being in that intimate relationship with God here and now as He guides, leads, and loves them. And then we need to tell them that they can go and spend forever with Him in heaven.

We and our children are born into a time when the most important thing is the spread of the Gospel. This is part of what God has for us, so your children need to develop the habit of going to God and saying, "Father, what is important to You right now is what is important to me. I know Your priority is spreading the Gospel. What can I do to help?"

Does this mean that we all must be in full-time ministry or be missionaries? No. We can be snowboarders and lawyers. But the focus in our lives should be to develop our talents and go where God wants us to go, laying down our lives for others. Our job is to bring a whole generation to Christ so that they can be with us in eternity.

God's individual plan for each of us is like a thread woven carefully and purposefully, in combination with many, many other threads, through the huge tapestry of His one big kingdom plan for spreading the Gospel to the world. If His plan is for Jamie to be a snowboarder and a lawyer, then Jamie's pursuing those callings is a key part of God's kingdom plan. Perhaps that is how God intends to draw those groups of people to Himself, or it might be His plan to light a lamp there that will shine and draw people to Him.

This higher calling, this hope of heaven and the spreading of God's kingdom, is all intertwined with His plans for us and our children. The threads of our lives, going where God has designed as we fulfill our calling and develop and use our talents, are an intimate part of the whole tapestry.

We can help our children prepare for this. We can teach them to pray for others and for the world. They should pray that God puts them not only in a place to develop their talents and grow in their relationship with Him but in a place where they can contribute to the growth of His kingdom on Earth.

God has given us life. As we give Him our lives He gives them back to us. This is an ongoing, continuous thing, so we need to instill in our children the desire to continually go to God, saying they want to make a difference here and now—in their professions, their families, their churches, and in the development of their talents and what He has called them to do, and through that, in the moving of the Gospel throughout the world.

This could happen in any number of ways. God might give them jobs where they could give extraordinary amounts of money. God might make them popular athletes and, through that, give them a platform from which they can speak to people about Jesus. They might become role models for others on a small or a large scale.

As God pours blessings into their lives, we need to show our children how to continually give back to God and keep asking God how they can give their time, talents, finances, and so on to bring others into God's kingdom. Our focus should be, "How can we get on Your agenda, God, and build Your kingdom?"

Help your children focus on the fact that it is not about having a happy little life here. It's really about developing who they are as the people God has made them to be so that they can walk into what God has for them in this time, this day, this world. It's about being able to walk into heaven and all that God has prepared for them for all of eternity. If this is their focus, they will have no trouble continually giving their lives back to God and laying their lives down for service for Christ and God's agenda day by day.

God knew in what age your children would live when He designed them and planned their lives, so your child's individual place and calling will match His kingdom plans. So, as another strong signpost, your children will find their calling while seeking God's higher calling.

"But seek first his kingdom and his righteousness, and all these things will be given to you as well" (Matthew 6:33).

1. Ask your child the following question: "If you could live a full life, when you get to heaven, what would you like to tell God you have accomplished?" This will give you an idea of what your child would like to do in life.

2. What is your children's idea of heaven? How well do they understand the link between what they do in this life and the possibilities in their eternal future? Assure them that heaven will fit them perfectly.

3. Do your children have a full awareness that God's present priority is spreading the Gospel? Ask them how they can share the love of Jesus where they are now and how their gifts and talents can be used for this purpose in the future.

4. Develop a plan together to pray for the salvation of those who interact with your children. Work with your children to think of a plan for how they can choose certain countries, people, or events to pray for over the next month.

5. Talk with your children about how their activities can be related to the second coming of Jesus. Tell them that God wants to use them in His great plan to bring Jesus back as the reigning King.

6. Ask your child if he or she understands the difference between being in the world—and even being able to enjoy some of what if offers—and being strangers in the world, not of it. How can your child be an ambassador from "another world" and yet resemble unbelievers in many superficial ways?

Appendix A

PERSONALITY TEST
FOR CHILDREN

Treasure Tree Personality Checklist

Is your child a Lion, Otter, Golden Retriever, or Beaver? What about you? Read the descriptions out loud. Put your child's or your initial by each description that is a consistent character trait. Total the initials for each personality. The larger numbers indicate basic personality traits.

Lion

1. Is daring and unafraid in new situations.
2. Likes to be a leader. Often tells others how to do things.
3. Ready to take on any kind of challenge.
4. Is firm and serious about what is expected.
5. Makes decisions quickly.

Total = _____

Otter

1. Talks a lot and tells wild stories.
2. Likes to do all kinds of fun things.
3. Enjoys being in groups. Likes to perform.
4. Full of energy and always eager to play.
5. Always happy and sees the good part of everything.

Total = _____

Golden Retriever

1. Always loyal and faithful to friends.
2. Listens carefully to others.
3. Likes to help others. Feels sad when others are hurt.
5. Patient and willing to wait for something.

Total = _____

Beaver

1. Is neat and tidy and notices little details.
2. Sticks with something until its done. Doesn't like to quit in the middle of a game.
3. Asks lots of questions.
4. Likes things done the same way.
5. Tells things just the way they are.

Total = _____

(Adapted from *The Treasure Tree*, © 1992 by John Trent and Gary Smalley)

Appendix B

PERSONALITY STYLE DISCOVERY EXERCISE FOR YOUTH

Personality Style Discovery Exercise

Work ➡ across ➡ each ➡ line ➡ from ➡ left ➡ to ➡ right!

Instructions: Rate each word using the scale below.

	1	2	3	4	5
SCALE:	Not At All Like Me	Not Very Much Like Me	Sometimes Not Like Me/ Sometimes Like Me	Like Me	Very Much Like Me

Put a **1, 2, 3, 4,** or **5** in the box next to **each word** as you move from ➡ **left to right.** ➡ Put a **1** for words that are *not at all like you*. Put a **5** for words that are *very much like you*. Put a **3** for words that could go either way—*sometimes not like you/sometimes like you*. Each line can have any combination of numbers. Example:

fearless	5	forceful	5	imaginative	1	encouraging	1	sociable	1	practical	3

➡ **Work across each line from left to right.** ➡

daring		take-charge		artistic		caring		friendly		organized	
adventurous		commanding		brainy		accepting		entertaining		detailed	
risk-taker		bossy		brilliant		agreeable		outgoing		practical	
competitive		controlling		clever		warm-hearted		sociable		achieving	
daredevil		independent		creative		encouraging		playful		prepared	
courageous		bold		imaginative		sensitive		loud		exact	
thrill seeker		forceful		inventive		pleasant		fun-loving		thorough	
fearless		decision maker		original		good listener		talkative		high standards	
driving		self-reliant		thinker		patient		noisy		productive	
pioneering		direct		witty		supportive		spirited		orderly	

Personality Style Discovery Exercise Scoring Sheet

1. Take hold of the *Personality Style Discovery Exercise*, page 183, on each side of the page, and pull the page up slightly until the bottom of the box is directly above the dotted line on this page. To protect your book, carefully turn under the bottom of the page without creasing it.

2. The six arrows should now line up with the six columns on page 183.

3. Add each column from top to bottom, entering the total for each column in its corresponding box on this Scoring Sheet (remember, there are six columns). Doublecheck your math by adding the columns again from bottom to top.

- -

place edge of exercise page here

	↑	↑	↑	↑	↑	↑
Add down TOTAL =	□	□	□	□	□	□
	ADVENTURER	**COMMANDER**	**CREATOR**	**ENCOURAGER**	**ENTERTAINER**	**ORGANIZER**

Add down TOTAL = (under each: ADVENTURER, COMMANDER, CREATOR, ENCOURAGER, ENTERTAINER, ORGANIZER)

4. When you've finished adding all six columns, find the column that has the highest score. In the event of a tie, select the one that seems the most like you (or that you like the most).

- Write the <u>Personality Trait</u> for your **highest** score here ↑ _____

5. Then, find the column with the **second highest** score.

- Write the <u>Personality Trait</u> for your **second highest** score here ↑ _____

Appendix C

PERSONALITY SURVEY FOR YOUNG PEOPLE AND ADULTS

Life Pathways

PO Box 1476, Gainesville, GA 30503
(770) 534-1000

Personality Survey

YOUR NAME: _____

DATE: _____

✦ Choose one of the following settings and give all your answers based on how you typically behave in that environment.

_____ natural behavior _____ work _____ marriage/home

✦ Rate each line of words from left to right on a 4, 3, 2, 1 scale with **4 being most** like you and **1 being least** like you.

You must use a different number (1, 2, 3, 4) in each column

↓	↓	↓	↓
_4_ Commanding	_1_ Enthusiastic	_3_ Loyal	_2_ Detailed

A - D	R - I	O - S	U - C
_____ Commanding	_____ Enthusiastic	_____ Loyal	_____ Detailed
_____ Decisive	_____ Expressive	_____ Lenient	_____ Particular
_____ Tough-Minded	_____ Convincing	_____ Kind	_____ Meticulous
_____ Independent	_____ Fun-Loving	_____ Peaceful	_____ Follow Rules
_____ Daring	_____ People-Oriented	_____ Understanding	_____ High Standards
_____ Risk Taker	_____ Lively	_____ Charitable	_____ Serious
_____ Courageous	_____ Cheerful	_____ Merciful	_____ Precise
_____ Confident	_____ Inspiring	_____ Supportive	_____ Logical
_____ Fearless	_____ Good Mixer	_____ Patient	_____ Conscientious
_____ Non-Conforming	_____ Talkative	_____ Gentle	_____ Analytical
_____ Assertive	_____ Popular	_____ Even-Paced	_____ Organized
_____ Take Charge	_____ Uninhibited	_____ Good Listener	_____ Factual
_____ Aggressive	_____ Vibrant	_____ Cooperative	_____ Accurate
_____ Direct	_____ Excitable	_____ Gracious	_____ Efficient
_____ Frank	_____ Influencing	_____ Accommodating	_____ Focused
_____ Forceful	_____ Animated	_____ Agreeable	_____ Systematic
_____ **TOTAL**	_____ **TOTAL**	_____ **TOTAL**	_____ **TOTAL**

Instructions

1. **Add the numbers in each column and plot the results as shown in the example below.** The points farthest to the left and right from the Mid-Range will have the greatest influence on your personality. Note in the example graph the person is (A) Adaptive, (S) Supportive, and (C) Conscientious.
2. **Identify your profile** (those points farthest from the Mid-Range).
3. **Use those points to confirm your strengths and weaknesses** listed on the back of this sheet. Those points falling in the Mid-Range will share characteristics of both ends of the dimensions. If all points are in the Mid-Range, you are either very versatile or experiencing some sort of transition in your life and should take the survey again at another time.

Example

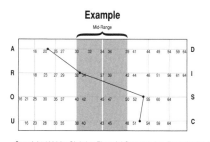

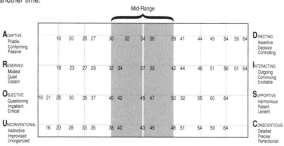

(over)

4/98

Typical Strengths and Weaknesses

The ADAPTIVE-DIRECTING dimension indicates the amount of control and decision-making authority desired.

Adaptive

STRENGTHS	WEAKNESSES
1. Adapt to other's agenda	1. Underestimate self
2. Cooperate	2. Not share opinions and judgments
3. Move slowly into new areas	3. Avoid taking charge
4. Be tactful	4. Not speak out
5. Focus on one thing at a time	5. Be overly sensitive, internalize criticism
6. Complete the current task	6. Lack assertiveness

Directing

STRENGTHS	WEAKNESSES
1. Set the agenda	1. Be a poor listener
2. Compete	2. Be insensitive to others
3. Move quickly to get results	3. Be impatient, critical
4. Be bold	4. Tend to overcommit
5. See the global perspective	5. Be demanding and pushy
6. Take on new challenges	6. Avoid routines and details

The RESERVED-INTERACTING dimension indicates the degree of social interaction desired.

Reserved

STRENGTHS	WEAKNESSES
1. Works alone or one on one	1. Be withdrawn, alone
2. Be serious	2. Appear secretive
3. Be practical	3. Be pessimistic
4. Not worry about what others think	4. Be curt
5. Be modest	5. Appear shy
6. Work quietly and listen	6. Drained by social contact

Interacting

STRENGTHS	WEAKNESSES
1. Meet new people	1. Avoid working alone
2. Be enthusiastic	2. Be uninhibited
3. Be optimistic	3. Be overly confident
4. Make a good impression	4. Need for approval
5. Be in the limelight	5. Be overly involved
6. Be talkative	6. Talk too much

The OBJECTIVE-SUPPORTIVE dimension indicates the degree of harmony/stability desired.

Objective

STRENGTHS	WEAKNESSES
1. Use logic over feelings	1. Be abrupt, restless
2. Be tough-minded	2. Be too critical
3. Be independent and self-reliant	3. Be suspicious
4. Manage conflict	4. Won't compromise
5. Be eager	5. Don't finish projects
6. Be dynamic	6. Be discontent

Supportive

STRENGTHS	WEAKNESSES
1. Be empathetic	1. Be too sensitive
2. Be warm, compasssionate	2. Be naive
3. Be supportive	3. Compromise too much
4. Promote harmony	4. Be afraid to confront
5. Be patient	5. Resist change
6. Be even-paced	6. Be complacent

The UNCONVENTIONAL-CONSCIENTIOUS dimension indicates the degree of structure/detail desired.

Unconventional

STRENGTHS	WEAKNESSES
1. Be spontaneous, unstructured	1. Be unorganized
2. Be flexible, versatile	2. Be undisciplined
3. Be unconventional	3. Be too informal
4. Work with concepts and generalities	4. Overlook important details
5. Rely on instincts	5. Be overconfident
6. Take a risk	6. Be too reckless, careless

Conscientious

STRENGTHS	WEAKNESSES
1. Be organized, structural	1. Be too picky
2. Be predictable	2. Be inflexible
3. Be conventional	3. Depend on rules
4. Work with specifics, details	4. Internalize emotions
5. Research for facts	5. Be a perfectionist
6. Take a cautious approach	6. Be overly analytical

NOTE: For more information on the DISC system, see *Finding the Career That Fits You* and *Your Career in Changing Times* by Lee Ellis and Larry Burkett, and *Understanding How Others Misunderstand You* by Ken Voges and Ron Braund. A more in-depth personality survey, *Personality I.D.,* is available from Christian Financial Concepts, 1-800-722-1976, or visit our Web site at www.cfcministry.org.

Christian
Financial
Concepts Inc.

Teaching | Biblical Principles of Managing Money

Larry Burkett, founder and president of Christian Financial Concepts, is the best-selling author of 50 books on business and personal finances. He also hosts two of CFC's four radio programs broadcast on hundreds of stations worldwide.

Larry earned B.S. degrees in marketing and in finance, and recently an Honorary Doctorate in Economics was conferred by Southwest Baptist University. For several years Larry served as a manager in the space program at Cape Canaveral, Florida. He also has been vice president of an electronics manufacturing firm. Larry's education, business experience, and solid understanding of God's Word enable him to give practical, Bible-based financial counsel to families, churches, and businesses.

Founded in 1976, Christian Financial Concepts is a nonprofit, nondenominational ministry dedicated to helping God's people gain a clear understanding of how to manage their money according to scriptural principles. Although practical assistance is provided on many levels, the purpose of CFC is simply *to bring glory to God by freeing His people from financial bondage so they may serve Him to their utmost.*

One major avenue of ministry involves the training of volunteers in budget and debt counseling and linking them with financially troubled families and individuals through a nationwide referral network. CFC also provides financial management seminars and workshops for churches and other groups. (Formats available include audio, video, and live instruction.) A full line of printed and audio-visual materials related to money management is available through CFC's materials department (1-800-722-1976) or via the Internet (http://www.cfcministry.org).

Life Pathways, another outreach of Christian Financial Concepts, helps teenagers and adults find their occupational calling. The Life Pathways *Career Direct* assessment package gauges a person's work priorities, skills, vocational interests, and personality. Reports in each of these areas define a person's strengths, weaknesses, and unique, God-given pattern for work.

Visit CFC's Internet site at http://www.cfcministry.org or write to the address below for further information.

Christian Financial Concepts, Inc.
PO Box 2377
Gainesville, GA 30503

Editing:
Adeline Griffith
Christian Financial Concepts
Gainesville, Georgia

Text Design:
Ragont Design
Rolling Meadows, Illinois

Cover Design:
The Puckett Group
Atlanta, Georgia

Printing and Binding:
Lake Book Mfg.
Melrose Park, Illinois